Computer Supported Cooperative Work

Series editor
Richard Harper, Social Shaping Research, Cambridge, United Kingdom

The CSCW series examines the dynamic interface of human nature, culture, and technology. Technology to support groups, once largely confined to workplaces, today affects all aspects of life. Analyses of "Collaboration, Sociality, Computation, and the Web" draw on social, computer and information sciences, aesthetics, and values. Each volume in the series provides a perspective on current knowledge and discussion for one topic, in monographs, edited collections, and textbooks appropriate for those studying, designing, or engaging with sociotechnical systems and artifacts.

Titles published within the Computer Supported Cooperative Work series are included within Thomson Reuters' Book Citation Index.

More information about this series at http://www.springer.com/series/2861

Gerhard Leitner

The Future Home is Wise, Not Smart

A Human-Centric Perspective on Next Generation Domestic Technologies

 Springer

Gerhard Leitner
Interactive Systems Research Group
Alpen-Adria-Universität Klagenfurt (AAU)
Klagenfurt, Austria

ISSN 1431-1496
Computer Supported Cooperative Work
ISBN 978-3-319-36582-4   ISBN 978-3-319-23093-1 (eBook)
DOI 10.1007/978-3-319-23093-1

Springer Cham Heidelberg New York Dordrecht London

Printed on acid-free paper

Springer International Publishing AG Switzerland is part of Springer Science+Business Media (www.
springer.com)

Preface

Although it happened a reasonably long time ago I remember it like it was yesterday. At the end of the 1980s in my first years of studying, I was with friends at a Chinese Restaurant in Vienna (well, it wasn't traditional, but it was economical). We were talking about our future plans. At this time I was an undergraduate student of psychology and therefore sort of knowledgeable in that area and, on an amateur level, a passionate computer user. When it came to discussing my future plans, I talked about my concern that, even though I love computers, the ones that were available seemed to completely ignore the psychological characteristics and human capabilities and limitations I had learned about in my studies. Computers seemingly did not deal with human capabilities, aspects of information processing, motivation, emotion, group phenomena, etc. I considered this a great opportunity for my professional future, to work on these drawbacks and so combine my professional and personal interests. A few years later, this *dream* became reality. In a lecture called "computer psychology", I was exposed to human-computer interaction and the CHI movement, which was quite new then. I have stayed in the field ever since. Retrospectively, the restaurant where it all began might be considered CHI-nese.

Like many other researchers in the field, I started with Desktop HCI (GUI and web). I observed the developments of theoretical HCI and of its application in the usability engineering movement, and I tried to make humble contributions to their progress. Over the years I came across both positive and negative aspects that were developing along with HCI. One positive aspect is that HCI has come to be commonly accepted as an important issue in computing, one that it should be considered in the development of every computing system which involves users – which is to say – in the development of almost every computing system. This, without question, led to many positive developments. For example, consider the current generations of mobile devices. In contrast to early computers, they are suitable for the masses and reflect some of the achievements of HCI.

A negative aspect in this regard is that, in becoming a little *natural*, HCI lost focus. Usability is now taken for granted – as is demonstrated in advertisements and brochures which misuse usability as a pure selling proposition – in some cases with questionable accuracy. The importance of facing new challenges with appropriate company of HCI has lost its focus. One of the effects is an increase in the number of problems caused by inappropriate technology – for example, with navigation devices that do not appropriately consider the driver's limited capabilities while driving. I would compare the situation to the proliferation of diseases and epidemics such as measles and polio. Some of them were considered exterminated but they have mutated and recently appeared again because of sloppy observation of appropriate vaccination and other preventive means. In my opinion, some areas of HCI are in a danger of suffering the same fate. Old interaction *diseases*, once considered exterminated, are now afflicting us again. One specific area where this is the case is the home, where bad HCI and usability *viruses* have a long tradition – just consider the VCR. These viruses are regaining strength over a huge number of different channels. The progress in technology (in the form of miniaturization, increased performance, and falling prices) supports these developments and increase the threat. New problems arise in the context of the roles technology is expected to assume in the future, such as the increasing age of the general population, the digital divide, and issues of energy consumption. The first time I observed the industry and media proclaiming a golden age of smartness, I was skeptical that these things could work out in such a simple way, and I think I was right. Although much research has been done in that area, there is still a long way to go. This book constitutes the final step in a long investigation into the field of HCI in general and, for the last few years, into the topic of smart homes in particular. It summarizes my work in several aspects in this field and attempts to develop a new paradigm in domestic technology ⇒ *The* WISE *home*.

St.Veit an der Glan, Austria   Gerhard Leitner
July 12, 2015

Acknowledgements

First of all I want to thank my wife Sonja and my children Elke and Anja, my mother Anneliese, and my father Johann who passed away a few years ago. Thanks also to the other members of family and friends who stood behind me in the years when the research for this book was conducted. From those people who supported me in my work, the first person I want to thank is Prof. Martin Hitz who hired the *alien* psychologist in his research group on the department of computer sciences. He made possible and supported the work for more than a decade which finally resulted in this book. My thanks also go to Prof. Alexander Felfernig, who also supported me over the last years in a wide variety of uncountable situations. Thanks also to my former and current students who were persistent enough to make the fantasies and imaginings of a trained psychologist a digital reality and who made possible the research on the WISE home presented in this thesis. A specific role in this group was played by Anton J. Fercher and John N.A. Brown, who not only did excellent work toward their respective graduations but also were very supportive and dear colleagues over the last years. My thanks go also to those colleagues with whom I shared my daily worries and led many productive discussions, specifically David Ahlström. Specific thanks go to those colleagues who represent the research background I originally came from, the humanities (psychology and sociology), Prof. Judith Glück[1] and Oana Mitrea. Special thanks to Chitra Hapsari Ayuningtyas whose contributions helped to bring the platform to the next level of maturity with her goal of researching multi-user scenarios. My thanks also go to the following students who contributed in different roles and from different perspectives to the further development of the WISE idea: Christian Lassen, Paul Czech, Thomas Lübbeke, Julia Schaar, Daniel Felsing, Wolfgang Rabl, Martin Florian, Beate Grötschnig, Sudheer Karumanchi, Rene Samselnig, Simona Jammer,

---

[1]Who, as a renowned wisdom researcher also inspired me to the idea of labeling my approach the WISE home.

Bettina Schmidt, Jaqueline Kueschnig, Martina Soldo, and Matthias Pum. I also want to thank the participants, partners and supporters of the projects mentioned in this book. Last but not least I want to thank the people at Springer, Beverley Ford, James Robinson and Sathiamoorthy Rajeswari for their support in the production phase of this book.

Prologue

A "smart" birthday story.

Some years ago I was participating in an event where an extended family met to celebrate a 30th birthday. Technology played an important role in the celebration, but it did so in a manner nobody would have anticipated. This example illustrates the weaknesses of the technology that is typically present in an average home and points forward what it would take to make it really smart.

In the late afternoon, all of the family members (13 adults and four children) met in the living room. Because of the special event, additional devices were present, enhancing the technical equipment that is typically available. In summary, there were several digital cameras, a video camcorder, a dozen smartphones, a musical keyboard, a laptop, a TV, a VCR, and a DVD player present in the room. After the meal the guests started chatting about this and that, and the discussion came around to a holiday trip that one couple had taken a few weeks earlier. Of course the couple was prepared to show pictures. However, as is usual nowadays, the pictures were not available as a physical photo album, but only on the storage card in one of the digital cameras. Now the task was to figure out how to manage to present the pictures to the whole audience in a way that would be more comfortable than either (1) crowding around the small screen or (2) passing the tiny camera from person to person. The display device of choice would have been the TV set because of its screen size, but the specific cable which could have connected the camera directly to the TV had been forgotten at home, and the TV did not have a slot for storage cards. The second idea was to burn the photos from the storage card onto a DVD; however, the DVD player was not able to play still pictures. To shorten the story, a chair was placed on the table and the laptop which did, fortunately, have a storage card slot was put on the chair. The photos were presented as a slideshow on the laptop screen. In this way the audience could see the photos simultaneously. Despite of all the technology present, the experience was anything but smart.

Contents

Part I
The Current State in Smartness

Chapter 1
WISE: The Difference Between Smart and Smart Ass

For if every instrument could accomplish its own work, obeying or anticipating the will of others, like the statues of Daedalus, or the tripods of Hephaestus which, says the poet, of their own accord entered the assembly of God. If, in like manner, the shuttle would weave and the plectrum touch the lyre without a hand to guide them, chief workman would not want servants, nor masters slaves.

Aristotle, *Politics* - from the translation by Benjamin Jowett [1]

The most profound technologies are those that disappear. They weave themselves into the fabric of everyday life until they are indistinguishable from it.

Mark Weiser, *The Computer of the 21st century* [2]

About 2300 years lay between these two quotes. Although they stem from different eras, they both illustrate the wish of humans to enhance their quality of life by means of appropriate tools and technologies. Tools have supported and extended human capabilities and helped to overcome limitations since the beginning of mankind. This is observable in relics of ancient times such as the *oldowan* [3]. In the year 2015, the endeavour to domesticate tools has still not come to an end. In recent decades a new category of technology, computing, has become ubiquitous and offers hitherto undreamed new possibilities to enhance each and every area of life, also in the home. Specifically the possibilities of *anticipation* emphasised by Aristotle are closer to become a reality than ever. However, the home constitutes a specific – and at the same time difficult – field in regard to tools and technology, because it has so many facets and serves multiple purposes and so requires the same of the tools available in it. As computing technology has started its triumphal march in other domains [4] it has still not optimally adapted to the home context. Many hurdles must be overcome before Weiser's vision of interwoven technology becomes reality. People spend about 70 % of their life time in their respective homes [5] and there is a great potential for the enhancement of life in the home with the support of technology that is capable of taking over responsibility, enables automation and anticipates user needs. But compared to other areas of life, the potential problems are just as great – as illustrated with the birthday story in the prologue. The inherent complexity and multi-dimensionality of the home requires

© Springer International Publishing Switzerland 2015
G. Leitner, *The Future Home is Wise, Not Smart*, Computer Supported
Cooperative Work, DOI 10.1007/978-3-319-23093-1_1

a different perspective on the relationship between the environment, the tools and basic (computing) technologies, and their users; one that goes beyond the purely technocratic relationship which has been predominant in the smart home field for decades, both in industry and in research and development.

As an example, the slogan of the 1933 World's Fair – "*Science finds, industry applies and man conforms*" [6] reflects such a technocratic perspective. Despite the long time that has passed, parts of that philosophy can still be identified in today's smart technologies. In some form of technologies the specific circumstances of the home seem to be completely ignored. Neither the process of developing technologies nor their use is unidirectional, but reciprocal. This was expressed by John Culkin's saying *First we shape our tools and thereafter they shape us* [7]. Reciprocity is a characteristic not only in regard to tools but also in regard to dwelling, the relationship between humans and the home as whole, as Winston Churchill said in a speech that may have inspired Culkin: "*We shape our dwellings, and afterwards they shape us*".[1] Even simple tools, such as those from the Oldowan period have been shown to have such shaping power. This was illustrated by [8] who showed that over the course of about 1 million years, the central part of the human hand has evolved an extra bone to adapt to this tool. But also the tools themselves have changed and have been re-shaped by generations of users. Because of their long time periods, evolutionary developments are difficult to observe and comprehend. Compared to the tools from the Oldowan, computing technology has a short history. As a result, long term effects cannot yet be fully estimated. But when observing, for example, the respective and obvious impacts television, the internet or mobile devices had and still have on human behaviour [9], the long term impacts can be assumed to be high. However, a big disadvantage of today's tools based on computing technology is the limited number of ways in which they can be *shaped* by their users. We are missing the reciprocity described by Culkin, and, in the case of home technology, by Churchill.

The inherent complexity of the home one the one hand and the limitations of current technologies on the other are probably one reason why the concept of the smart home, has, since its introduction in the middle of the 1980s [10], been promised many times, but still has not become as popular as expected. The spread of technology that would deserve to be called *smart* in terms of being able of dealing with and appropriately adapting to such complex circumstances still lays far behind expectations on the private home sector, even though it was fairly successful in the industrial and public sectors [11, 12]. Today so many things are labelled *smart*. Smart TVs, smart phones, smart cars are only a few examples and the list could go on and on. It is therefore necessary to delimit the characteristics of smartness that will be addressed in this book.

The starting point of a large scale contention with smart technology in industry and academia was the coining of the term *smart home* in 1984 [10]. This was the first external sign of the endeavours to ring in a new age of technology [13].

---

[1]Speech, Oct. 28, 1944, House of Commons.

Since then many terms denoting smart technology have entered our language, such as *intelligent home, smart living, domotics, home of the future, networked home, internet of things,* or *robotics* [13–15]. The basic technologies can be applied in very different areas, for different purposes and in different building types. Because of the variety of applications and meanings of *smart* the research presented in this book is focused on the private home. This focus is necessary due to the inherent differences between private living environments and all of the environments and circumstances designated for other purposes (such as workspaces, public places, the outdoors, etc.). For example, private homes and workspaces are distinct when considering the factors influencing the adoption, acceptance and use of technology. The term *smart home* as used in this book is meant as an umbrella term synonymous to the terms enumerated above and focused on the context of private dwellings. The functional range of such smart technology is, for example, defined by [16, 17] who link smart technologies to the ability to integrate and network devices and to provide *intelligent functionality*. The most current forms of smart technologies are based on artificial intelligence [18, 19] and labelled *ambient intelligence* (AmI) *systems* [19].

One reason for the reluctance of humans to adopt such ambient technologies in their homes is probably the emphasized inherent but typically uni-directional *shaping power* of this type of technology and the degree to which it is interfering with daily life. In a typical home, Television, DVD players or household appliances are relatively wide-spread as stand-alone devices, although attempts to network these kinds of devices are increasing. Technology that assumes an integrative and connecting role and is, in the words of Weiser *interwoven*, is potentially more difficult to understand and to control. Given the long-term experiences that consumers have with relatively *harmless* technology, it is easy to understand related fears. An example of that kind of harmless technology, as provided by Norman [20], has achieved sad notoriety. He tells the story of an event in 1990 in which the former president of the United States, George Bush, Sr., articulated the following vision. *"By the time I leave office I want every single American to be able to set the clock on his VCR"*. Twenty years later, Norman [20] provided a succinct comment on this vision – *"he failed"*. The impact of a VCR on daily life is negligible, so long as we disregard simple annoyance. The potential consequences of smart technology that does not work in the expected way are observable in many examples and are no longer only relevant for techies but have reached public attention [21].

The situation described in the birthday story in the prologue includes a collection of problems that result from trying to use current technology in the home. Most of the devices in the example could be considered as kind of *smart*. They have a level of computational power that we could not have dreamed of a few years ago. They have capabilities and were designed to fulfil the needs required in the example – dealing with pictorial content. In fact, many devices with appropriate displays were present. Missing interface standards and issues of interoperability and integration meant that users could not *shape* functionality to their needs. As a result, the available *smartness* was useless. This is when technological features are apparently developed from the limited viewpoint of technical capabilities and not from the perspective of user needs. To describe it with the words of [22], the devices can be considered ego-centric. Unfortunately, citizens of the so-called developed world are used to such technology-related problems, but it is understandable that their level of frustration about a questionable *smartness* increases.

It was the contrast between the ambitious industry and media forecasts on the one hand and the insights gained from real world observation on the other that inspired me to take up the smart home in a scientific manner. The followed approach is built upon Shneidermans [23] call for a paradigm shift in the domain of computing; exchanging the old computing (which was about what computers can do) for a new computing (which would be about what humans can do). In the same way, this book introduces a paradigm shift in home technology; away from the smart home centred on technological capabilities, and towards a WISE home that is about what humans need to enhance their living experience.

The paradigmatic change is necessary because in contrast to, for example, mobile devices, state-of-the-art home *smartness* obviously did not convince a reasonable percentage of people to adopt it into their daily lives. This is probably because the basic technology has proven to be less *smart* than "*smart ass*" [21]. As a result the attribute *smart* has developed negative connotations, specifically in the context of home technology. For example, *smart metering* has come to be associated with spying on people and abusing access to their personal data rather than to benefit from more efficient energy control. Such negative associations with the attribute *smart* do not only come to mind in regard to technology but also in regard to smart people. This assumption is based on an observation made by Sternberg [22], who could show that smart people are particularly susceptible to negative personality traits such as egocentrisum, delusion of omniscience, omnipotence and invulnerability. Some characteristics of smart homes have similarities to these traits. A variant of ego-centrism was illustrated by the birthday story. Another example is what Nielsen [24] at the end of the 1990s labelled as "*remote control anarchy*" representing a variant of ego-centrism conveyed by the manufactures of these devices. Some kind of omniscience-thinking is identifiable in a story depicted by [25] in which a smart home system switched off the lights (because it was the usual time for that) even though people were still sitting in the living-room. I witnessed a similar situation in a newly-built living lab in Germany. When the highly-sophisticated smart home system changed the lights without user request, one of the researchers responsible for the system turned to me and said: "Ich möchte hier nicht wohnen" (I would not want to live here). The message these kinds of smart home systems convey to the customers has frightening parallels to the *man conforms* philosophy. Humans would have to adapt their requirements to the capabilities of the technology, in most cases even brand specific ones. The basic operation mechanisms and interfaces are the only appropriate solution and competing products based on alternative usage patterns are doing wrong. As a result, any expectations or user habits that deviate from the features offered by that particular technology must also be wrong [5]. The solution is to broaden the perspective on the problem to one that goes beyond smartness.

1.1 Introducing the WISE Paradigm

The reason the new paradigm is labelled WISE and not, for example, *smart 2.0*, is to clearly convey a difference to the *"Man conforms"* [6] philosophy which is based on the self-conception that people would have to adapt to the features the technology offers. The result is depicted in Fig. 1.1 – humans imprisoned by the technology. Human computer interaction, which is one of the theoretical foundations of this book, proposes the evidently more appropriate approach of adapting technology to human capabilities. But as pointed out in the preface, HCI seems to have disappeared from the focus of attention. Introducing the new paradigm should contribute to re-gaining the attention again HCI deserves.

As an analogy to human development, where wisdom is considered a stage beyond intelligence, WISE aims at going beyond smart; overcoming the shortcomings of current smart technology as impetus for further research and development [26]. The WISE approach is built upon the characteristics of human wisdom, and as defined [22]:

> ...the application of intelligence, mediated by values, toward the achievement of a common good, through the balance among intrapersonal, interpersonal and extrapersonal interests, over the short and long terms, to achieve a balance among adaption to existing environments, shaping of existing environments and selection of new environments [22].

Wisdom does not have negative connotations in either its scientific or everyday use. This is what makes WISE different. In this sense the positive association with WISE is intended to be a message; a sign for potential users that a different approach to technology is possible. It might help to change the negative attitude to smart technology in general and to the smart home in particular. To be able to achieve this, WISE must be more than just another new label. The WISE home is designed as both a theoretical concept and a novel research approach.

The basic theoretical concept constitutes a combination of two dimensions, as illustrated by its acronym: **W**isdom-**I**nspired,**S**mart-**E**nhanced. The first dimension is devoted to a thorough consideration of human capabilities (wisdom-inspiration). The second, to enhanced smartness; building upon the capabilities of smart home technology with a focus on advanced possibilities of computing, such as Artificial

Fig. 1.1 The situation in a state-off-the-art smart home – the human is a prisoner of technology

Intelligence (AI). The goal is at once simple and difficult. The simple part of the equation is helping people to achieve *a good life*. This is closing the circle between Aristotelian philosophy ("*eudaimonia*"), the work of Weiser and current approaches in research which also focus on the *good life* aspect, such as positive psychology [27, 28]. The difficulty is illustrated by a quote from Weiser's influencial paper, to achieve this good life by … *technologies that fit the human environment instead of forcing humans to enter theirs.*

WISE is an attempt to broaden the perspective on technology in the home in order to overcome the gaps in current home technology that have already been discussed. My background in psychology and my work in computer science (or more precisely HCI) provides an optimal starting point for this attempt; addressing the problem by following a human centric approach [29]. A progress in smart technology is not only relevant to the personal goal of achieving a good life, but also to what the European Union has labelled the *societal big challenges* [30, 31]. Challenges that are related to this book can be labelled as the triple E (Elderly, Energy, and, Effectuation). Technology in the private home will play significant role in meeting these challenges, but only once consumers are convinced of the benefits of adopting it into their day-to-day lives and enabled to appropriately use them.

- **Elderly** – Numerous publications and statistical estimations, cf. e.g. [32], show the rapid approach of major demographic changes. A shrinking group of working adults is confronted with a continually growing cohort of the elderly. This leads to bottlenecks in care and support due, for example, to a shortage of qualified personnel in nursing and healthcare. Smart home technology is often praised as a kind of panacea that might resolve the coming problems. Considering the example given in the birthday story in the prologue; who would want to be dependent on such technology for their health care, much less in a life or death situation?
- **Energy** – Scarce resources, specifically dwindling fossil fuel, are forcing large-scale changes in economy and politics. The increased participation of private households in energy issues is inevitable, because they are responsible for around 40 % of the energy consumption [18]. Different forms of participation are already going on and more can be anticipated. Smart metering can be seen as of some kind of participation, though a rather involuntary and passive one. Metering alone would not lead to the expected effect. Active forms of participation would be necessary addressing the intrinsic motivation of consumers and include conscious and voluntary behavioural changes in order to sustainably reduce energy consumption. These can be, for example, reducing standby energy or increasing the consciousness of device use. To achieve this, the possibility of *shaping* technology according to the consumers' needs has to be made available by appropriate means of observation, intervention and correction.
- **Effectuation** – It is necessary to reduce costs specifically in times of economic crisis. Companies and public authorities are therefore constantly searching for possibilities of cost reduction. One solution is the replacement of expensive offline-services with slim and cheap online self-service. As a result, people

are increasingly confronted with digital interfaces to governmental, medical or financial services. People who are not able to deal with these changes are in the danger of becoming victims of the digital gap. The need for self-services and the need for self-maintaining and administering computing technology will also increase in other domains. In this sense [33] predict an age of systems that are *easy to develop* following the age of *easy to use*. But, as shown in the birthday story, even the preceding age has not fully been reached yet. The active contribution to computing technology in the home (similar to the Web 2.0) will therefore require adequate means of interaction as well as a re-consideration of basic human requirements and needs. As Davidoff [25] formulated it, the focus has to be clear: *"People do not want to control devices, they want to have better control of their lives."*

The home constitutes a central point in life and plays an important role on a personal and societal level. People spend a significant amount of time in their homes [5, 16], with the goal of leading a good life; a goal that is both simple and difficult to achieve. Everything that contradicts this overall goal in the long term will probably not succeed. People will only accept technology if it is useable; if it has understandable practical benefits or supports attitudes and values either on the individual or on the societal level. After decades of home technology that is about half smart, it is now time to fill the smart home with a new spirit. In this sense, the old smartness, which is often not observable, accessible or comprehensible has become outdated and a new approach needs to be undertaken.

However, it has to be clear that the goal of WISE is not to make technology artificially WISE. A similar attempt with intelligence in the past was only partly successful. WISE aims at enhancing technology in a way that it is capable of behaving in a WISE way such that it cooperates with its human users. In contrast to a smart(ass) home, which overexerts or overrules, the WISE home acts and reacts like a thoughtful granny observing her grandchildren; giving them support when they need it, but letting them experiment and explore in order to learn how to interact with and control the world around them. The primacy of WISE is that technology adapts to the humans and the prevalent environmental conditions, and not the other way around. This book is both a summary of previous research work, and an initial step towards the new paradigm. It aims for the identification of a possible avenue for further development of private living environments.

In Part I of this book the current chapter and Chaps. 2 and 3 provide an overview of motivation and the theoretical backgrounds upon which the WISE approach has been built. Chapter 2 is devoted to the basic theoretical concepts, with HCI as the central foundation and those human aspects that are considered as specifically relevant in the interaction with smart homes. The notion of the home, its meaning as a central place in life and its facets is addressed in Chap. 3.

Part II of the book starts with a historical discourse of technology in the home in Chap. 4, from ancient times until the present era of the smart home and points out those aspects which are most relevant in regard to the WISE home. Chapter 5 presents a basic framework of WISE derived from the theoretical considerations of

Part I. The framework allows for a smooth integration of two principle forms of interaction: explicit interaction (related to HCI) and implicit interaction (related to AI, AmI). Chapter 6 is devoted to the methodological approach to be followed to empirically investigate the WISE concept, with an emphasis on fieldwork. The lead concept of the approach is user experience, but other concepts will also be presented.

The final part, Part III, starts with the presentation of examples for an empirical proof of the WISE concept in Chap. 7 corresponding to the three stages of developments, presented in Chap. 5. The final chapter, Chap. 8 provides an estimation of how the home of the future may look like, and why it should be WISE.

References

1. Aristotle. (350 B.C.) Politics. The justification of slavery (B. Jowett, Trans.). http://socserv. mcmaster.ca/econ/ugcm/3ll3/aristotle/Politics.pdf.
2. Weiser, M. (1991). The computer for the 21st century. *Scientific American, 265*(3), 94–104.
3. Stout, D. (2011). Stone toolmaking and the evolution of human culture and cognition. *Philosophical Transactions of the Royal Society B: Biological Sciences, 366*(1567), 1050–1059.
4. Hindus, D. (1999). The importance of homes in technology research. In *Cooperative buildings. Integrating information, organizations, and architecture* (pp. 199–207). Berlin/Heidelberg: Springer.
5. Hamill, L. (2003). Time as a rare commodity in home life. In *Inside the smart home* (pp. 63–78). London: Springer.
6. Pursell, C. W. (1979). Government and technology in the great depression. *Technology and Culture, 20*, 162–174.
7. Culkin, J. M. (1967). A schoolman's guide to Marshall McLuhan. *Saturday Review, 50*, 20–26.
8. Ward, C. V., Tocheri, M. W., Plavcan, J. M., Brown, F. H., & Manthi, F. K. (2014). Early Pleistocene third metacarpal from Kenya and the evolution of modern human-like hand morphology. *Proceedings of the National Academy of Sciences, 111*(1), 121–124.
9. Ling, R. (2004). *The mobile connection: The cell phone's impact on society*. Burlington: Morgan Kaufmann.
10. Harper, R. (2003). *Inside the smart home*. London: Springer.
11. Dietrich, D., Bruckner, D., Zucker, G., & Palensky, P. (2010). Communication and computation in buildings: A short introduction and overview. *IEEE Transactions on Industrial Electronics, 57*(11), 3577–3584.
12. Marinakis, V., Doukas, H., Karakosta, C., & Psarras, J. (2013). An integrated system for buildings' energy-efficient automation: Application in the tertiary sector. *Applied Energy, 101*, 6–14.
13. Chan, M., Estève, D., Escriba, C., & Campo, E. (2008). A review of smart homes – Present state and future challenges. *Computer Methods and Programs in Biomedicine, 91*(1), 55–81.
14. Venkatesh, A., Dunkle, D., & Wortman, A. (2011). Family life, children and the feminization of computing. In *The connected home: The future of domestic life* (pp. 59–76). London: Springer.
15. Ricquebourg, V., Menga, D., Durand, D., Marhic, B., Delahoche, L., & Loge, C. (2006). The smart home concept: Our immediate future. In *2006 1ST IEEE International Conference on E-Learning in Industrial Electronics* (pp. 23–28). Piscataway: IEEE.
16. Alam, M. R., Reaz, M. B. I., & Ali, M. A. M. (2012). A review of smart homes – Past, present, and future. *IEEE Transactions on Systems, Man, and Cybernetics, Part C: Applications and Reviews, 42*(6), 1190–1203.
17. Aldrich, F. (2003) Smart homes: Past, present and future. In R. Harper (Ed.), *Inside the smart home* (pp. 17–39). Berlin/Heidelberg: Springer.

18. Cook, D. J. (2012). How smart is your home? *Science (New York, NY), 335*(6076), 1579.
19. Ramos, C., Augusto, J. C., & Shapiro, D. (2008). Ambient intelligence – The next step for artificial intelligence. *IEEE Intelligent Systems, 23*(2), 15–18.
20. Norman, D. A. (2010). *Living with complexity*. Cambridge/London: MIT.
21. Iovine, J. (2000). When smart houses turn smart aleck. *New York Times, 13*. http://www.nytimes.com/2000/01/13/garden/when-smart-houses-turn-smart-aleck.html
22. Sternberg, R. J. (2003). *Wisdom, intelligence, and creativity synthesized*. Cambridge/New York: Cambridge University Press.
23. Shneiderman, B. (2003). *Leonardo's laptop: Human needs and the new computing technologies*. Cambridge: MIT.
24. Nielsen, J. (2004). Remote control anarchy. Jakob Nielsens Alertbox.
25. Davidoff, S., Lee, M. K., Yiu, C., Zimmerman, J., & Dey, A. K. (2006). Principles of smart home control. In: *UbiComp 2006: Ubiquitous computing* (pp. 19–34). Berlin/Heidelberg: Springer.
26. Herczeg, M. (2010). The smart, the intelligent and the wise: Roles and values of interactive technologies. In *Proceedings of the First International Conference on Intelligent Interactive Technologies and Multimedia* (pp. 17–26). New York: ACM.
27. Staudinger, U. M., & Glück, J. (2011). Psychological wisdom research: Commonalities and differences in a growing field. *Annual Review of Psychology, 62*, 215–241.
28. Baltes, P. B., & Staudinger, U. M. (2000). Wisdom: A metaheuristic (pragmatic) to orchestrate mind and virtue toward excellence. *American Psychologist, 55*(1), 122.
29. Bannon, L. (2011). Reimagining HCI: Toward a more human-centered perspective. *Interactions, 18*(4), 50–57.
30. Friedewald, M., Costa, O. D., Punie, Y., Alahuhta, P., & Heinonen, S. (2005). Perspectives of ambient intelligence in the home environment. *Telematics and Informatics, 22*(3), 221–238.
31. European Union. Societal Changes. http://ec.europa.eu/programmes/horizon2020/en/h2020-section/societal-challenges.
32. Eurostat Population Statistics. (2012). http://epp.eurostat.ec.europa.eu/statistics_explained/index.php/Population_structure_and_ageing.
33. Lieberman, H., Paternó, F., Klann, M., & Wulf, V. (2006). *End-user development: An emerging paradigm* (pp. 1–8). Amsterdam: Springer.

Chapter 2
Why Is It Called Human Computer Interaction, but Focused on Computers Instead?

This chapter is devoted to the basic scientific concepts and theories which serve as foundations for the WISE home. As has been pointed out in the previous section, my scientific background is in HCI. Therefore the following argument will be built upon that.

2.1 Human Computer Interaction and WISE

Human computer interaction (HCI) as defined by [1] is

> ...the discipline concerned with the design, evaluation and implementation of interactive computing systems for human use and with the study of major phenomena surrounding them.

HCI can be considered responsible for building the bridge between the technology present in the home and the inhabitants. Characteristics of the interface are in the central focus of HCI in general but particularly so in the context of the home [2]. The interface connects the technical system and the user, and it therefore has a potentially big impact on the success and failure of the *human-machine system* as a whole [3]. Raskin was underlining the importance of the interface by saying that as far as the customer is concerned, the interface is the product [4, p. 5]. One of the general motivational arguments of this book is that technology in general and computing technology in particular have received more attention in the past, and aspects of the human user are not appropriately considered.

A change of the perspective from technological to human aspects is necessary. For a better understanding, we use a concept that can be seen as the least common denominator of the related disciplines, which is the information-processing approach. HCI shares a common history with cognitive psychology. Key people worked in both areas or in cooperating research groups. For example, Allen Newell was renowned in the related research areas. It is therefore not surprising

© Springer International Publishing Switzerland 2015
G. Leitner, *The Future Home is Wise, Not Smart*, Computer Supported
Cooperative Work, DOI 10.1007/978-3-319-23093-1_2

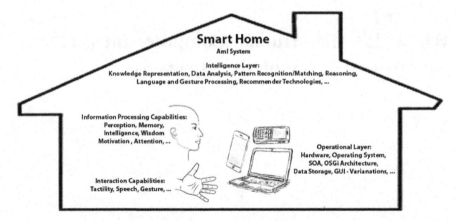

Fig. 2.1 The model shows a variation of the original HCI Model of the ACM [1], emphasizing the differences of the interaction between a smart home and a human. On the left hand side the human is depicted, which is characterized by input (vision, hearing), processing (thinking, reasoning) and output capabilities (tactility, speech). On the right hand side exemplary devices a smart home offers to interact with it. Above the user and the explicit devices available in the home the ambient infrastructure which integrates, for example, a knowledge base and artificial intelligence features that support the interaction between humans and the smart home

that the information-processing approach, which superseded the stimulus-response and behaviourist models, has been adopted in cognitive psychology and HCI. Information processing is, in simplified terms, characterized by input, processing and output capabilities. These three parts can serve as the basis for a comprehensive and easy description of the technical system as well as a simplification of the processes going on in side of the human user. Moreover this approach simplifies the identification of potential problems and the areas that are related to these problems. The Model Human Processor introduced by [5] was historically one of the most influencial models to describe the basic procedures and steps that occur in human computer interaction on the basis of this information processing approach. The model depicted in Fig. 2.1 constitutes a derivate of the original HCI model [1] adapted to the smart home context and emphasizing its specifics. The model is an attempt to illustrate the interaction between a user and a smart home system. The main difference to the original HCI model is that the machine part of the system (at least some of its components) surrounds the human user.

2.2   The Technological Part of a Smart Home

Before going into more detail on the human aspects that are considered relevant for the WISE home, a short overview of the machine part in general and the specifics of smart home technology in particular is given. The computer or machine part in the original nomenclature of the ACM SigCHI consists of, in a simplified and abstracted view, input and output components (labelled C1 in the original overview

[1]) representing the hardware part of the system, and features which describe the software components responsible for communicating with the human users, subsumed under the term dialogue principles (labelled C2 to C5 [1]). Already on these aspects a computerized home has a much higher variability than, for example, a desktop computer. Understanding relevant aspects and influencing factors requires a broader perspective.

Input devices in a smart home can vary widely. The simplest category are physical devices such as wall switches which consist of a hardware based interface that enables a limited number of states (e.g., boolean on/off). On the other end of the spectrum, complex virtual devices such as smart phones, tablets or wall-mounted panels integrate a large number of basic logic operations enabled by software interfaces. Inbetween the two extremes we find a broad variety of devices which, for example, represent *internet of things* [6], characterized by a potentially arbitrary combination of hard- and software components. A user would use very different devices and flexibly choose locations to trigger actions in the system, for example, to switch on a light. This triggering process involves very different steps and procedures on the technical and interactional level. The borders between input/output and dialogue features are, in comparison to the original definition and to the interaction with stand-alone computers, blurred and much more complex. When considering the interaction between a computerized system and a human as a sequence, then the next step would be the evaluation of the consequences an input has caused. The evaluation should be supported by features of the system. Examples for such features have been enumerated by Norman [7] which are, for example, feedback, mapping, constraints. Feedback that corresponds to an interaction with a conventional *everyday thing* [7] or with a conventional computer typically appears on the same location where a trigger was issued. A user can see the system reaction, for example, by showing the hourglass until the system responds by starting a program. With conventionally equipped homes this is similar. When a light switch is pressed the light bulb starts to glow in the same room and feedback is observable immediately. There were already exceptions of this immediacy in the past. For example, when light switches mounted indoors are responsible for controlling external lights. These simple changes make potential problems obvious. Figure 2.2 shows scenes I frequently come across; buildings where outside lights are glowing during the day – probably because of suboptimal feedback on the location where the trigger happened.

Fig. 2.2 Lanterns switched on during day time

In conventional computing there has been a continual increase in the number of devices that were remote from the location of their controls. In office environments, for example, where printers are not in the same room as the computers. Direct feedback like the sound of the printer was not observable any more, but was simulated on the desktop. In the context of the smart home, devices that are remote controlled have become the standard with the effect that direct feedback is no longer available. Turning on lights from the smart phone or from a smart switch requires appropriate feedback to the triggering person. Different modalities on the input as well as on the output level further increase the complexity. This small excursion shall point out the potential complexity and problems of interaction in a smart home. But despite of a wide body of literature pertaining to smart home control systems these and other even basic HCI aspects are not appropriately considered in current smart home systems. One of the reasons for this shortcoming is, beside others, a limited focus in related research. A query in the databases of IEEE, Elsevier or ACM reveals a few thousand of smart-home related publications. However, a recent meta analysis by [8] points out that the majority of related research is focused on technical aspects. One conclusion the authors draw is that "... *the smart living domain is still a domain of technicians, and therefore the technical-related challenges have a higher priority.*" Also earlier publications [9–13] come to the conclusion that there is too a strong focus on technology and technological solutions in related research. The result is a *technology push* [8, 11, 12, 14] rather than demand or *user pull* [15], sometimes even a disregard of user interests [16]. One episode that illustrates the problem happened when I gave one of my talks. I was presenting results achieved and the data generated within the project described in more detail in Chap. 7. The work I was presenting was attacked by a man who worked in the area of theoretical informatics and simulations. He specifically criticised the amount of data that had been collected. In his opinion my datapoints were miniscule. He pointed out that within simulations multiples of millions of datapoints can be generated in a fraction of the time the field study I presented lasted. Obviously there is still a lack of understanding that there are aspects to be considered relevant beside the current hype of big data. As will be discussed in more detail in Chap. 6 it is important that smart home research goes beyond simulations in artificial circumstances.

The focus on technical aspects in the main stream of smart home research does not mean that the HCI community completely ignored the developments. Work addressing the potential dangers and challenges of the smart home is observable for quite a long time, but did not seem to get attention in the degree the technological aspects did. Critical voices on the smart home from the perspective of HCI appeared shortly after the concept of the smart home was announced. In 1985 [7] sketched those developments more as a threat than an opportunity. A general criticism expressed, for example by [17] is that instrumental aspects in general dominate HCI, which is particularly problematic in regard to the smart home. As will be pointed out in detail in Chap. 6 the design and evaluation of basic interaction mechanisms has been done under quite artificial circumstances. The results that were achieved are questionable. This development was certainly not the original objective of the ACM SigCHI, as observable in the original publication [1]. Another source of information that supports this view is the first author of the work, Tom Hewett himself, whom I had the honour to meet at the end of the 1990s in Vienna when he stayed with my institute as a guest professor. He always motivated the students, mainly students of computer science, to consider human aspects in computing to a higher extent. He did the same within instructive and inspiring conversations with us staff members, showing us the variety of aspects of cognitive psychology and their potentials in HCI. The following section shines a light on some of them.

2.3 Shining a Light on Human Aspects

It would be beyond the scope of this book to go into detail about the entire human characteristics that would be relevant to a smart home. General characteristics of the information processing approach have anyway been addressed in numerous publications covering basics of perception, characteristics of memory, thinking or problem solving and output capabilities such as tactility, speech or gestures, for example [18, 19]. These basics will therefore not be repeated at this point. The following sections are focused on those human capabilities which are considered just as important, particularly in regard to the smart home, but which, for several reasons did not receive the attention they deserved [1, 3]. The first section addresses the two dimensions which are of central importance in the reasoning of this book: intelligence and wisdom. The former, more precisely its synonym *smartness*, is the starting point of the problems addressed in this book and the latter is serving as the eponymous concept of the new paradigm to be achieved.

2.3.1 Shining a Light on Intelligence

The term intelligence is used in different scientific disciplines with different meanings. Because of that this section starts by clarifying those differences. Artificial intelligence (AI) as the first concept to be addressed, constitutes a central element of today's smart environments and addresses the capabilities of computers to assume intelligent behaviour. Ambient intelligence (AmI) is considered the state-of-the-art evolutionary step of AI [2] and covers computational capabilities that characterize smart environments [2, 20] the smart home is one of which. AmI makes possible [2] "... *aiming at a proactive, but sensible support of people in their daily lives*" by providing the following exemplary functions: AmI environments are able to interpret the state of the environment they are integrated in; they can represent information and knowledge associated with the environment; model, simulate and represent virtual entities (*agents*) in the environment; plan decisions; and plan and execute actions. These functions are achieved by the combination of *operational technologies* [2] (basic hardware such as sensors and actuators) and AI. The latter enables advanced forms of interaction between humans and the technical system and constitutes an indispensable part differentiating AmI from conventional smart technology. However, in the impression of [2] AmI is often build without AI, concentrated on operational technology and therefore is not able to provide the advancements AI would be capable of.

Like AI and AmI, human intelligence (HI) has many facets and there are many theories which define human intelligence from different perspectives. Theories that define HI with psychometric aspects, focus on intelligence measurement. Multi-factorial models of intelligence differentiate between different dimensions of intelligence. Others define intelligence based on developmental aspects, and there are also biologically-oriented theories. A statement of [21] illustrates the inherent problem to find a common definition of intelligence. They argued that the number of definitions one can get is equal to the number of intelligence theorists that are asked. However, a common definition exists that is satisfactory for our purposes. It defines human intelligence as "…the ability to understand complex ideas, to adapt effectively to the environment, to learn from experience, to engage in various forms of reasoning, to overcome obstacles by taking thought. Those abilities will vary on different occasions, in different domains, as judged by different criteria [21]."

This definition of HI includes parallels to and differences from AI and AmI and also shows the potential conflicts between intelligent technology and intelligent users. The form of intelligence (AI, AmI) that represent the technological view do, for example, not only integrate human intelligence as a cohesive phenomenon but partly integrate also other elements of human information processing. Those parts are in the perspective of HI separated from the concept of intelligence. Interaction problems are probably related to the differences in the perspectives of the related scientific disciplines and differences in the features and behaviours of the technical system and the human. The effect is a conflict between the machine and the user caused by the multiple intelligences present (AI, AmI and HI). Taking into consideration the notion of wisdom may possibly offer a means of overcoming these problems.

2.3.2 A Spotlight on Human Wisdom and Its Potential to Improve Smart Homes

As with the multiple theoretical backgrounds of intelligence, there are also many different approaches that address wisdom. The orientation followed in this book is based on the definition by [22] who defines wisdom

> …as the application of intelligence and experience, mediated by values toward the achievement of a common good through a balance among intrapersonal, interpersonal, and extrapersonal interests, over the short and long terms, to achieve a balance among adaptation to existing environments, shaping of existing environments, and selection of new environments…, …the individual applies tacit and formal knowledge to seek a common good.

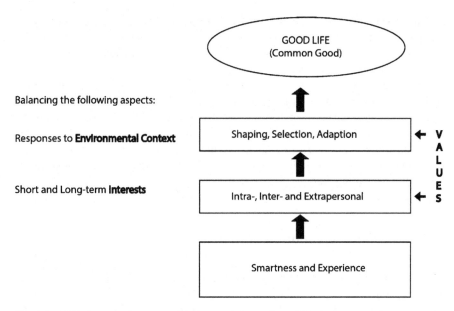

Fig. 2.3 A Wisdom based concept of the home (Adapted from [22])

The components of [22]'s wisdom model are depicted in Fig. 2.3.

There are some aspects included in the definition of wisdom which could help to overcome problems and enhance the interaction with smart technology in the home; simply put: to make it WISE. In the same way as a WISE human, the WISE home applies intelligence and experience, which means that it is based on intelligent features (such as reasoning) and gains experiences by the collection and analysis of data. In this way it can learn from situations that it has observed before. Data and algorithms derived from those analyses are stored and can be retrieved again from a knowledge base. Not only individual data are collected to identify habits and routines, but also multi-user behaviours are considered and automated functions can be derived to support the achievement of a common good. The common good in this context is, following Aristotelian philosophy and positive psychology, "*a good life*". Wisdom is observable in different aspects. One is that the storage and retrieval of data can be considered an aspect of wisdom, tacit knowledge in the sense of [22] which is applied to resolve a potential problem. The application of this form of knowledge means that the WISE home is not only relying on an explicit trigger by a user, but can derive a solution from past behaviour. The other aspect of wisdom is the consideration of values. Values can be observed as being static as well as dynamic rule systems characterizing a specific environment. A real smart, or even WISE, home has to be able to deal with such values. This is achieved by continually referring to the knowledge base in order to reason what is best representing the value system of a certain environment at any given moment and whether there are any conflicts. Another facet of wisdom is that if the WISE home identifies a potential change, it does not stubbornly perform a function, but is able to negotiate the performance with the human user. The final aspect of wisdom is the consideration of information from the outside world. Knowledge derived from this source of information can be considered a variant of wisdom of the crowds [23], fulfilling different purposes than knowledge generated inside the home. For example, with collaborative filtering generalizable data (e.g. weather forecasts) can be used to enhance the performance of a heating system without the need of explicit interaction by a user. However, the most important requirement is that users must always have the possibility of manual override [24]. This is necessary to prevent inhabitants from, as has been illustrated on the examples given in Chap. 1, smart(ass) technology overruling them.

2.3.3 Shining a Light on Attention

Another dimension of human information processing that would deserve more interest specifically in the settings of the home, is attention. When taking into consideration Weiser's demand for "*technologies that disappear*", it is not understandable that today's technologies are typically pushing themselves to the fore. For example, GPS navigation devices in cars are considered responsible for a high percentage of traffic accidents because of their distractive features [25, 26]. In a current household, technology is often also designed on this kind of misunderstanding of attentive capabilities which fortunately do not (yet) have such dramatic impacts, but are at least leading to unnecessary annoyance. The many devices present in a conventional home are competing for the attention of their owners, typically with enervating signals [27]. In our frequent discussions on the smart home, my boss Martin H. always refers to his tumble dryer. When it has finished the drying cycle it informs the environment about this state with a continuous and frequent "*Beeeep!*" which only would stop when someone pressed a button on it. Martin always finishes the story by saying: "*If I had a gun, I would shoot the dryer*".

As any technology is potentially disruptive [28], and the number of devices in a home continuously increases, a re-orientation is required, appropriately considering the circumstances where a system is used [15, 29] and taking into account the variety of human capabilites. Smart technology it its current form has the danger that things that were hitherto in the background and should stay there now come into the foreground. This is specifically observable with mobile devices that almost clutch their users and let them forget their surroundings [30]. The WISE approach takes into account alternatives, such as what [3] emphasized. One of them is to focus on peripheral attentive mechanisms. As an example, the concept [31] of calm computing could be a WISE alternative to intrusive technology with a specific benefit in the smart home context. Technology that is based on supporting peripheral attention [31] could enhance interaction in the home, examples such as the Dangling String are given by [31] and can also be found in our own work [32].

2.3.4 Shining a Light on Human Needs and Motivation

The last dimension that is addressed in this section is motivation. Its relevance in the context of the smart home is manifold. Motivational aspects are driving human behaviour in very different ways, for example in the form of motivations or needs. A stronger consideration of human needs in the context of smart homes is frequently demanded in the related literature, for example [7, 11, 14, 33, 34]. Dewsbury [35] citing Quigley and Tweed states that: "*Visions of what technology is... ... are rarely based on any comprehensive understanding of needs and in some cases are blatant technology push*". An important question to answer is what kind of needs and in what form they could be considered in the context of the smart home? At this point two exemplary approaches are presented which cover different motivational aspects considered relevant. The first example is addressing motivation aspects accompanying the usage of smart home technology and the potentials of this kind of technology to fulfil or support the fulfilment of human needs. The theory of Maslow [36] became important in psychology and other scientific disciplines and also has been influencial in HCI. According to the model, needs are organized into a hierarchical order of relative prepotency. A simplified principle of the hierarchy is that needs of a lower level have to be fulfilled to a certain extent before needs of an upper level become the focus of interest. *Physiological needs* represent the basic level of the model and are responsible for achieving a *homeostasis*, involving body functions such as breathing, nutrition, and, sexual activities. These needs are the predominant ones and are prioritized over others. When they are fulfilled to a certain extent, the next level, *security needs*, become relevant. These include the need of security of body and life, including *feeling safe*, in a familiar context or environment. The next level, *love needs*, involve social belonging, to a family, to groups or to the society. The fourth level is *self-esteem needs* which are described as being satisfied with one's own achievements and being respected by relevant others. The needs of these first four levels are summarized as deficiency needs, whereas needs of the next and final level – the need for self-actualization – is defined as growth need. It is different to the other need categories because it can never be fully fulfilled.

The other approach presented consists of a group of theories originating from Fishbein and his colleagues [37] and can be labelled as the *reasoned action approach*. The basic elements the theories are based on differ form the concepts of Maslow. The basic assumptions can help, for example, to understand the motivational aspects that are related to the decisions to adopt smart technology or not. Utility and usability (described in detail in Chap. 6) play a role in this regard as well as the influence of other people (subjective norm). The approach has been influencial in HCI in the form of the technology acceptance model (TAM).

Both theoretical approaches presented serve as a basis for the WISE approach. Considering the variety of needs and motivations, it seems more understandable that people are motivated to apply some smart home functionalities but do not want to apply others. What could, for example, be the needs involved when controlling blinds in the home with the smart phone? If the motivation is that the sun blinds the eyes, then physical needs are relevant. When the reason is because one is afraid of burglary, then safety needs are active. In both cases the utility of a behaviour and the usability of the process that leads to a result are important. In another context, when showing the feature of remote control to friends, love needs and self-esteem may play a role, as well as the subjective norm. Those differences are appropriately addressed by the WISE home to help people to fulfill different needs in an appropriate way. The fulfilment of the basic needs shall *just work* and not be complicated by technology. As [24] pointed it out with the expressions of participants interviewed regarding smart technology *"Things must be simpler to do than in a normal house ... I don't want to work through a menu just to turn off the lights"*. Other activities serving the fulfilment of self-actualizing needs based on computers, televisions, smart phones, in general, may be less problematic. These hypotheses are less based on theoretical consideration, but have been derived from empirical work that was carried out in the context of the WISE approach and presented in Chap. 7.

The WISE concept and the components addressed in this chapter constitute parts of a conceptual model which requires additional empirical proof. Therefore it is based on assumptions and components the actual relevance of which cannot be fully specified. It is clear that the basic theories presented are subject of controversy and it has to be pointed out that there is no claim for completeness in the concepts that are potentially relevant in the context of home. The selection is, however, not arbitrary, but includes those concepts that have been addressed in our empirical work and that have resulted at least partly, in empirical proof.

References

1. Hewett, T. T., Baecker, R., Card, S., Carey, T., Gasen, J., Mantei, M., & Verplank, W. (1992). *ACM SIGCHI curricula for human-computer interaction*. New York: ACM.
2. Augusto, J. C., & McCullagh, P. (2007). Ambient intelligence: Concepts and applications. *Computer Science and Information Systems, 4*(1), 1–27.
3. Carroll, J. M. (Ed.). (2003). *HCI models, theories, and frameworks: Toward a multidisciplinary science*. San Francisco: Morgan Kaufmann.
4. Raskin, J. (2000). *The humane interface: New directions for designing interactive systems*. Reading: Addison-Wesley Professional.
5. Card, S., Moran, T., & Newell, A. (1986) The model human processor. In K. Boff, L. Kaufman, & J. Thomas (Eds.), *Handbook of perception and human performance* (Vol. 2, pp. 1–45). New York: Wiley.
6. Atzori, L., Iera, A., & Morabito, G. (2010). The internet of things: A survey. *Computer Networks, 54*(15), 2787–2805.
7. Norman, D. A. (1988). *The psychology of everyday things*. New York: Basic Books.
8. Solaimani, S., Bouwman, H., & Baken, N. (2011). The smart home landscape: A qualitative meta-analysis. In *Toward useful services for elderly and people with disabilities* (pp. 192–199). Berlin/Heidelberg: Springer.
9. De Silva, L. C., Morikawa, C., & Petra, I. M. (2012). State of the art of smart homes. *Engineering Applications of Artificial Intelligence, 25*(7), 1313–1321.

10. Alam, M. R., Reaz, M. B. I., & Ali, M. A. M. (2012). A review of smart homes – Past, present, and future. *IEEE Transactions on Systems, Man, and Cybernetics, Part C: Applications and Reviews, 42*(6), 1190–1203.
11. Chan, M., Estéve, D., Escriba, C., & Campo, E. (2008). A review of smart homes – Present state and future challenges. *Computer Methods and Programs in Biomedicine, 91*(1), 55–81.
12. Aldrich, F. (2003). Smart homes: Past, present and future. In R. Harper (Ed.), *Inside the smart home* (pp. 17–39). London/New York: Springer.
13. Yamazaki, T. (2006). Beyond the smart home. In *International Conference on Hybrid Information Technology, 2006 (ICHIT'06)*, Jeju Island (Vol. 2, pp. 350–355). IEEE.
14. Haines, V., Mitchell, V., Cooper, C., & Maguire, M. (2007). Probing user values in the home environment within a technology driven Smart Home project. *Personal and Ubiquitous Computing, 11*(5), 349–359.
15. Rode, J. A., Toye, E. F., & Blackwell, A. F. (2004). The fuzzy felt ethnography-understanding the programming patterns of domestic appliances. *Personal and Ubiquitous Computing, 8*(3–4), 161–176.
16. Eckl, R., & MacWilliams, A. (2009). Smart home challenges and approaches to solve them: A practical industrial perspective. In *Intelligent interactive assistance and mobile multimedia computing* (pp. 119–130). Berlin/Heidelberg: Springer.
17. Hassenzahl, M., & Tractinsky, N. (2006). User experience-a research agenda. *Behaviour and Information Technology, 25*(2), 91–97.
18. Preece, J., Rogers, Y., Sharp, H., Benyon, D., Holland, S., & Carey, T. (1994). *Human-computer interaction*. Wokingham/Reading: Addison-Wesley Longman.
19. Dix, A., Finlay, J., Abowd, G., & Beale, R. (2004). *Human-computer interaction*. Harlow: Pearson Education Limited.
20. Cook, D. J., & Das, S. K. (2007). How smart are our environments? *Pervasive and Mobile Computing, 3*(2), 53.
21. Neisser, U., Boodoo, G., Bouchard, T. J., Jr., Boykin, A. W., Brody, N., Ceci, S. J., & Urbina, S. (1996). Intelligence: Knowns and unknowns. *American Psychologist, 51*(2), 77.
22. Sternberg, R. J. (2004). What is wisdom and how can we develop it? *The Annals of the American Academy of Political and Social Science, 591*(1), 164–174.
23. Surowiecki, J. (2005). *The wisdom of crowds*. New York: Anchor.
24. Hamill, L. (2006). Controlling smart devices in the home. *The Information Society, 22*(4), 241–249.
25. Swanson, B.-M. http://www.automotive-fleet.com/fc_resources/af1010-safety-20-distracted-1.pdf.
26. Jensen, B. S., Skov, M. B., & Thiruravichandran, N. (2010). Studying driver attention and behaviour for three configurations of GPS navigation in real traffic driving. In *Proceedings of the SIGCHI Conference on Human Factors in Computing Systems (CHI '10)*, Atlanta (pp. 1271–1280). New York: ACM. doi:10.1145/1753326.1753517. http://doi.acm.org/10.1145/1753326.1753517.
27. Harper, R. (2011). *The connected home: The future of domestic life*. London: Springer.
28. Edwards, W. K., & Grinter, R. E. (2001, January). At home with ubiquitous computing: Seven challenges. In *Ubicomp 2001: Ubiquitous computing* (pp. 256–272). Berlin/Heidelberg: Springer.
29. Oudshoorn, N., Rommes, E., & Stienstra, M. (2004). Configuring the user as everybody: Gender and design cultures in information and communication technologies. *Science, Technology & Human Values, 29*(1), 30–63.
30. Ling, R. (2004). *The mobile connection: The cell phone's impact on society*. Burlington: Morgan Kaufmann.
31. Weiser, M., & Brown, J. S. (1996). Designing calm technology. *PowerGrid Journal, 1*(1), 75–85.
32. Brown, J. N. A. (2014). *Unifying interaction across distributed controls in a smart environment using anthropology-based computing to make human-computer interaction "Calm"*. Ph.D. thesis, Erasmus Mundus Doctorate Program in Interactive and Cognitive Environments (ICE), Alpen Adria Universität Klagenfurt, Austria.

33. Barlow, J., & Gann, D. (1998). A changing sense of place: Are integrated it systems reshaping the home? http://139.184.32.141/Units/spru/publications/imprint/sewps/sewp18/sewp18.pdf.
34. Harper, R. (Ed.). (2003). *Inside the smart home*. Berlin/Heidelberg: Springer.
35. Dewsbury, G. (2001). The social and psychological aspects of smart home technology within the care sector. *New Technology in the Human Services, 14*(1/2), 9–17.
36. Maslow, A. H. (1943). A theory of human motivation. *Psychological Review, 50*(4), 370–396.
37. Ajzen, I. (2012). Martin Fishbein's legacy the reasoned action approach. *The Annals of the American Academy of Political and Social Science, 640*(1), 11–27.

Chapter 3
The Different Meanings of Home

Mid pleasures and palaces though we may roam,
Be it ever so humble, there's no place like home;
A charm from the sky seems to hallow us there, Which,
seek through the world, is ne'er met with elsewhere.
Home, home, sweet, sweet home!

Home Sweet Home by John Howard Payne, 1882[1]

The dissemination of automation technology stayed behind expectation in private home. Some of the potential reasons for this were addressed in the introduction chapter and in the previous chapter which turned a spotlight on the human aspects that would have to be considered to a higher extent. This chapter is devoted to the characteristics and the relevant aspects of the home environment, and its relationship to the people living and acting in it.

3.1 The Dimensions of Home

The following presentation of historical and trans-disciplinary perspectives on the home is serving as another basis of the WISE home. One important aspect to start with is the differentiation between the terms home and house. In the smart home literature, specifically in the technology-oriented parts of it, the terms are often used interchangeably. As Dekker [1] emphasises, it is important to make a clear distinction between them, although the borders between the two terms are fluent. The term house covers only the physical characteristics of a *"spatial unit in the built environment"* [2]. The archetype of the house, crystallized with the ascent of the bourgeois, is a free-standing house with a yard, occupied by a single family. The labelling of house as a castle, which is still used in the saying *"my home is my castle"* today, originates from these times, when the British law included passages such as *"The Englishmen's house is his castle, home as haven comprising both house*

[1] http://www.stthomassalisbury.co.uk/content/pages/documents/1295352003.pdf

© Springer International Publishing Switzerland 2015
G. Leitner, *The Future Home is Wise, Not Smart*, Computer Supported
Cooperative Work, DOI 10.1007/978-3-319-23093-1_3

and surrounding land." [2, p. 65] and defined the idealized form of dwelling. This type of living environment constituted a *"badge of the middle class membership"* for a long time [9] and housing statistics reveal that this idealised picture of a dwelling is still representative today. For example, in 2012 [3] about 41 % of Europeans lived in flats, but the majority of living environments still correspond to the ideal (34 % live in detached and 24 % in semi-detached homes) coined in the past, though the concrete percentages differ between countries. Physical characteristics are by far not the only relevant ones in regard to a home, however they are influential [2]. Beside the *"outer shell"* of a house, room design and furnishing, and the technology present in a house all enable and constrain behaviour, actions, and relationships, in the sense of "*... buildings that shape us*" as Churchill expressed it.

The outer shell of a house serves an important role as borders, it enables a separation between public and private, and contributes to making the home a comfortable, secure, and safe space. The house constitutes a refuge, a haven [4], a shelter [5] wherein one is removed from public scrutiny and surveillance [2, p. 71]. Public spaces serve non-kin relationships, the home is characterized by close and caring relationships [6]. The notion of *home* includes, beside the physical ones, also psychological, cultural, normative, moral, and social aspects. Moore [7], citing Benjamin 1995, defines home as:

> ... spatially localized, temporally defined, significant and autonomous physical frame and conceptual system for the ordering, transformation and interpretation of the physical and abstract aspects of domestic daily life at several simultaneous spatio-temporal scales, normally activated by the connection to a person or community such as a nuclear family.

In this interpretation the home is considered an entity interwoven with its inhabitants to such a degree that a separation between the two components, seems *fictious*: *"self and world merge in the activity of dwelling"* [6]. A similar understanding of the home is found in the work of the philosopher Heidegger [8]. The specific relationship between people and their homes can be observed in the etymological emergence of the words related to dwelling. The word *building* has its origin in the Germanic word *buam* – which is synonym to dwelling. Dwelling is seen as the sheer representation of being of *"us mortals"* in the world. The meaning of "*I am*" is, "*I dwell*" [8].

Whereas the type of dwelling has, as emphasized above, a historical relevance on the societal level, the home has an important individual historical perspective. It is not only that the current home is *shaping* life, homes of the personal history are all associated with memories [2]. The birthplace home plays a specific role in this regard [1, 7, 9]. Not all associations with home are positive, as is the case for people who have been abused or mistreated [10]. These kind of things often happen in the seemingly-protected environment of the home, but, fortunately, for most of us the home is one *"the most cherished place"* [2].

Compared to other places, such as working spaces, the home is differently organized. For example, when the home is built, designed or re-designed, the foremost consideration is not for the workflow that will take place. Besides the functional aspects, the home is also organized on aesthetic aspects, practical considerations, economic aspects or moral principles [6] that support the manifold purposes the home has to serve. Whereas workplaces are associated with clearly-defined tasks flows, the home is characterized by unplanned and parallel activities, unclear procedures, and changing roles [11]. Other goals are relevant at home. Consider, for example, efficiency. While this plays an important role in work contexts, it is *overrated* [12] in the home. In principle, at home there are no external role expectations [5]; responsibilities and task allocations are not so clearly specified as they are in the workplaces, and they may change depending on current requirements. Despite that freedom and flexibility, changes in society and technical progress forced changes upon role models and expectations. One example of this is gender. The roles of women in general and as technology consumers in particular has risen up, and women continue to play an important role in this regard [13]. This focus persists, specifically with technology aimed at supporting household chores [14], which make the home a women's workplace or even a *"girl's prison"*, as G.B. Shaw put it. Despite the clear focus of women as the user, most technologies are still being designed by men. Conventional technologies as well as smart home technologies are also usually established by men and overlook women. The work of [15–18] show that this is still the case in other areas of application and in different cultures.

The complexity of the home. which can only be addressed at this point on a very superficial level, is difficult to grasp. Rybczynski [19] describes it like an onion. In appears simple on the outside but has many layers the complexity of which are not observable from outside. If each layer is observed separately, sight of the whole is lost. It seems that this is exactly what has happened in the history of home technology: the layers of the home have been separated, and researchers have been focussing too much on the technical layer instead of concentrating on the *big picture*.

An indicator supporting this assumption is given by [20] who points out that the diffusion of technology led from the workplace to the home. It can be hypothesised that this has been done by extracting technology from the original context and deploying it to the new one. That this strategy does not work can be observed on several examples in the past, when plants and animals (such as the Japanese knotweed) were unreflectedly exported to other regions of the world. The consequences were not observable and the whole ecosystem has been disturbed. As has been mentioned in the introduction, such long term consequences of technology are not observable yet. But a thorough understanding of the context the technology is deployed can probably prevent negative consequences.

However, the criticised deployment strategy is partly understandable, specifically from an economic viewpoint, because it supports the requirements of a technology-oriented engineering approach such as standardization, replicability and configurability. The approach has its eligibility, specifically in industrial settings. In order to ensure criteria such as efficiency and effectiveness, buildings in the industrial or in the public sector are designed on the basis of these requirements. Floor plans are organized on the basis of repetitive patterns and rooms are prepared for standard installations. Such standardization enhances the effectiveness and efficiency when buildings have to be equipped with electrical power, heating, sanitary installations, and also smart technology. Moreover, the maintenance, control and regulation of the technical infrastructures can be handled more efficiently when based on standardized patterns instead of on individual solutions or custom designs. People responsible for the selection, the planning and the purchase of these infrastructures are probably not their users. The same applies to computerized equipment and software. Specific staff is available to handle initial configuration and ongoing maintenance in a centralized way. People staying in the buildings, for example, for the purpose of working, probably do not have an influence on the purchase, installation, and finally, the use of smart home technology.

Automation technology attained a suitability for mass production after the pioneering work of the 1950s and 1960s, which will be discussed in detail in Chap. 4 and could be quite successfully introduced into the functional building sector. In these circumstances automation technologies supported the achievement of goals related to efficiency and effectiveness. For example, energy consumption can be optimized by automating the systems in the building in order to coordinate the control of temperatures, lighting conditions, standby energy consumption, etc. Another benefit is the enhanced maintainability. Janitors, administrators, and technicians can remotely observe departments, rooms, and singular devices; can identify errors, and might even be able to solve them remotely by controlling the whole system from their desk. But as, for example, pointed out by [21], even in these circumstances, the real procedures deviate significantly from their technical specification and characteristics of the users play an important role. This will be illustrated with two examples showing the potential problems of a too technology-oriented approach even in work environments.

The first example relates to a laboratory which is located in a multi-unit research park. Built quite recently, the park is equipped with smart technology which, in principle, should not be of direct interest for the people working there. An automation system is installed which enables the remote-control of all devices present in the buildings. One example is the external horizontal blinds that serve as window shutters. If they are angled towards the building when it rains, the rainwater will run into the building's facade, which may result in cosmetic or even structural damages. To prevent this, all of the building's shutters are adjusted automatically based either on weather forecasts or on information provided by sensors positioned on the roof of the building. As a result, people sitting in their offices sometimes see the shutters suddenly adjusting themselves as though they were being controlled by the hand of the ghost. Of course, these adjustments happened regardless of whether bright sunlight might currently disturb people trying to read on a monitor, or watch a projection in what had been a dark room. This strange behaviour of the blinds finally led to the demand that some of the tenants of the park wanted to have the blinds removed.

A colleague who knows that I am researching smart technology provided me with information about the experience of a smart system that is installed on a university campus that was recently built in another city. The negative highlights of a report summarizing the experiences with the smart system so far are the following. The central control of the smart system is an incapacitation of the users. Heat, which is provided individually on a room-by-room basis, cannot be controlled individually. As a result, room-by-room installations to regain control to a certain extent, such as devices for humidification, have been added by the people working in the buildings. Control of the lighting is also centralized, and the lights in each room are automatically adjusted based solely on daylight conditions. Users frequently ask for light switches to be installed, so that they can reclaim some individual control. Maintenance costs are high because the entire system needs to be reprogrammed each time even if only light bulbs are replaced. If a door malfunctions, attempts to adjust the central door locking system (which consists of 1200 doors) require up to seven specialists.

Given these examples it is more than questionable to transfer technology from the context of functional buildings to the context of private residential buildings. Despite of the dangers, attempts in this direction are observable again and again. Figure 3.1 contains an indicator of how the limited perspective described above results in suboptimal solutions. The first picture is the workplace of a technician; a janitor surveilling a building from a central position. The other picture shows a typical control unit of a smart home control system. Even though the context of use is very different, the two designs are obviously based on the same concept.

As stated above, in contrast to industrial and public buildings, living environments are characterized by a reasonable diversity. Even on the physical level they differ in room layout, although there are some similarities, for example in regard to the types of rooms that are typically present. Confusing the standardized requirements that apply to public buildings with the requirements that apply to the home obviously leads to problems. An example of a conflict between standardization and individualism is illustrated in a report about the LeCorbusier house in Berlin. The architect Le Corbusier's became famous for his concept of the *machine-á-habite* (machine to live in) [22] which is based on the assumption that living environments can be standardized and do not change over time. In the Berlin flat this was not the case. Over the years the life developed a new and unique dynamic, which was described by [23] as follows: *"Like moles the people have undermined the structures and re-designed them individually"*. The conclusion that [4] draws from this is that people do not want machines to live in, they want machines to live with. According to [5] research suggests that the concept of replication (an extension of the concept of living machines) does not match with people's meaning of *home*. It does not make sense to view the home with the lens of mass production, efficiency, and productivity. Approaches that follow this path have some parallels to Taylorism and the *man conforms* philosophy which were massively combated by psychologists such as Kurt Lewin, but do not seem to be exterminated yet. A home of the future, a WISE home has to be based on adaptive and flexible technology that supports current needs of the inhabitants, such as the possibility to design their environments

Fig. 3.1 Workplace of a person monitoring a complex environment and a typical smart home dashboard

themselves and can deal with the changes that will occur as a natural part of life [24]. These can be, for example, the progressing from single life to living as a couple, becoming a family with or without children, etc. Ingold ([6], p. 165) brings it to the point: "*Most fundamental thing about life is that it does not begin here or end there, but is always going on*" – circumstances that probably cannot be fully addressed by a pure engineering approach.

3.2 Bridging the Gap

Given the different perspectives addressed above – the individual perspective of the home with its variety of dimensions on one side and the industrial perspective of standardization on the other – they do not seem to have much in common. The first requires approaching the home from the viewpoint of the humanities: considering the historical, psychological, sociological and philosophical aspects. The second represents the industrial perspective from standardized buildings to home automation, emphasising the efficiency, maintainability and costs aspects.

The problem to overcome is that housing and dwelling are generic and objective and subjective and individual, all at once, and all in parallel [9]. Engineers seem to try to avoid the individual because of the difficulty of deriving common solutions in non-generalized environments, and the dangers that may result from the attempt. But what if the individual perspective is the important one? For each of us, dwelling is unique and experienced separately [9] and therefore it is difficult to fully understand the various needs and choices, the values, from an external and general perspective.

It appears to be quite difficult to combine the two perspectives within the home, but it may be easier than it seems. Standardization has become widespread, because it would be unrealistic to demand customised solutions for each and every home given the complexity and the costs that would result from this. We are all already living with standardisation in our homes, and if addressed appropriately, no general problems result from this. Electric wiring and connectors in homes have to be standardized, because of compatibility requirements of components produced by different manufacturers, so that they can be used in a variety of buildings, and under a variety of circumstances. Despite the variability of homes, the rooms and infrastructural elements such as doors or windows are standardised in a way to fit the *human size*. Despite this standardization, living environments allow for a sufficient degree of individualisation. Furniture can easily be bought off-the-shelf because, given that the measurements have been taking into appropriate consideration, one can safely assume that the standard piece will fit into the environment. Without such degrees of freedom, a certain furniture retailer from Sweden would not have been so successful. Products are obviously designed and produced with standardization in mind, but in a way that still leaves room for individualism. The concept of mass customization [25] is an approach that combines the both perspectives, individualism and standardization. Returning to the example of entertainment technology from the birthday story at the beginning of this book, one can clearly see the tasks that will need to be addressed in the future. In principle TV sets, DVD players, and satellite receivers of many different brands are compatible with one another in regards to their physical interfaces. The same applies to computing technology. Displays, printers, smart phones, and cameras can be connected to a desktop or laptop computer and will probably work, at least, after drivers have been downloaded. What is missing is the possibility on the software level that enables the combination and integration of devices that have come from different manufactures and that are based on different interaction patterns. The WISE approach addresses the problems and shows examples how to support consumers to configure and program their homes themselves.

References

1. Dekkers, W. (2009). On the notion of home and the goals of palliative care. *Theoretical Medicine and Bioethics, 30*(5), 335–349.
2. Mallett, S. (2004). Understanding home: A critical review of the literature. *The Sociological Review, 52*(1), 62–89.
3. Eurostat. European Household Composition Statistics. http://epp.eurostat.ec.europa.eu/statistics_explained/index.php/Household_composition_statistics.
4. Spigel, L. (2005). Designing the smart house Posthuman domesticity and conspicuous production. *European Journal of Cultural Studies, 8*(4), 403–426.
5. Takayama, L., Pantofaru, C., Robson, D., Soto, B., & Barry, M. (2012). Making technology homey: Finding sources of satisfaction and meaning in home automation. In *Proceedings of the 2012 ACM Conference on Ubiquitous Computing*, Pittsburgh (pp. 511–520). ACM.
6. Ingold, T. (2000). *The perception of the environment: Essays on livelihood, dwelling and skill.* London/New York: Routledge.
7. Moore, J. (2000). Placing home in context. *Journal of Environmental Psychology, 20*, 207–217.
8. Heidegger, M. (2009). Bauen, Wohnen, Denken. In M. Heidegger (Ed.), *Vorträge und Aufsätze* (11th ed., pp. 139–156). Stuttgart: Klett-Cotta.
9. King, P. (2004). *Private dwelling: Contemplating the use of housing.* London/New York: Routledge.
10. Perkins, H. C., Thorns, D. C., & Winstanley, A. (2002). *The study of "home" from a social scientific perspective: An annotated bibliography* (2nd ed.). Christchurch: University of Canterbury.
11. Davidoff, S., Lee, M. K., Yiu, C., Zimmerman, J., & Dey, A. K. (2006). Principles of smart home control. In *UbiComp: Ubiquitous computing* (pp. 19–34). Berlin/Heidelberg: Springer.
12. Bell, G., Blythe, M., & Sengers, P. (2005). Making by making strange: Defamiliarization and the design of domestic technologies. *ACM Transactions on Computer-Human Interaction (TOCHI), 12*(2), 149–173.
13. Rutherford, J. W. (2010). *Selling Mrs. Consumer: Christine Frederick and the rise of household efficiency.* Athens: University of Georgia Press.
14. Blythe, M., & Monk, A. (2002, June). Notes towards an ethnography of domestic technology. In *Proceedings of the 4th Conference on Designing Interactive Systems: Processes, Practices, Methods, and Techniques*, London (pp. 277–281). ACM.
15. Aldrich, F. (2003). Smart homes: Past, present and future. In R. Harper (Ed.), *Inside the smart home* (pp. 17–39). London/New York: Springer.
16. Oudshoorn, N., Rommes, E., Stienstra, M. (2004). Configuring the user as everybody: Gender and design cultures in information and communication technologies. *Science, Technology & Human Values 29*(1), 30–63.
17. Selwyn, N. (2007). Hi-tech = guy-tech? An exploration of undergraduate students' gendered perceptions of information and communication technologies. *Sex Roles, 56*(7–8), 525–536.
18. Wu, X. (2008). Men purchase, women use: Coping with domestic electrical appliances in rural China. *East Asian Science, Technology and Society, 2*(2), 211–234.
19. Spronk, B. (2006). Rybczynski, W. A house is not a home: Witold Rybczynski explores the history of domestic comfort. Aurora.
20. Hindus, D. (1999). The importance of homes in technology research. In *Cooperative buildings. Integrating information, organizations, and architecture* (pp. 199–207). Berlin/Heidelberg: Springer.

21. Suchman, L. A. (1987). *Plans and situated actions: The problem of human-machine communication*. Cambridge/New York: Cambridge university press.
22. Le Corbusier. (1931). *Towards a new architecture*. John Rodker, London.
23. http://www.tip-berlin.de/kultur-und-freizeit-theater-und-buehne/das-wort-haben-die-benutzer-im-corbusierhaus.
24. Yamazaki, T. (2006). Beyond the smart home. In *International Conference on Hybrid Information Technology, 2006 (ICHIT'06)*, Jeju Island (Vol. 2, pp. 350–355). IEEE.
25. Pine, B. J. (1999). *Mass customization: The new frontier in business competition*. Boston: Harvard Business Press.

Part II
The WISE Approach: From Sweet and Smart to WISE

Chapter 4
A Focused Survey on Technology: From Hypocaust to Smart Appliances

It is difficult to determine exactly when smartness came to be of interest for humans the first time, but it can be hypothesized that this interest is almost genetically anchored in humans. What is clear is that smartness in general and smart enhancements for living environments in particular are not an invention of the present. This is shown, for example, in the excerpt from Aristotle's politics that opened Chap. 1. Technology-based smartness for the living context was already available in the ancient world. For example, consider the smartness of systems to improve public health (canalisation), to enhance comfort (hypocaust heating, bagdirs), and even to serve as a form of entertainment. The last is seen on, for example, inventions that are attributed to Heron of Alexandria (called mechanicus) [1], who probably lived in the first century B.C. The following figure shows an example of smart technology that was in operation when Heron lived. It is a smart heating system used in ancient Korea that I had the chance to see during a visit to Seoul in 2010. The *ondol* constitutes a predecessor of modern waste heat utilization, intelligently re-using the heat that is produced when cooking (Fig. 4.1).

Centuries later, in the middle ages, da Vinci devoted parts of his innovation work to building technologies, as seen in his concepts for cities which can be considered *smart* in relation to the time in which Leonardo lived, and insofar can be observed as predecessors of today's smart cities [2]. In my observation, the work of de Caus [3] is specifically important in regard to smart homes. He presented a collection of *so wol nützlichen alß lustigen machiner* (useful as well as funny machines) [3] to the german prince-elector Frederick, the fifth. This was an outstanding pioneering work for smart home technology, as it was the first where two perspectives of smart technology were jointly considered – as expressed in the title; technology that supports the utility aspect on the one hand and technology supporting entertainment on the other.

This dichotomy accompanies people in their homes, and is also important in regard to other concepts addressed in this book. For example, in the notion of User Experience (UX), which emphasizes the importance of hedonic aspects in

© Springer International Publishing Switzerland 2015
G. Leitner, *The Future Home is Wise, Not Smart*, Computer Supported
Cooperative Work, DOI 10.1007/978-3-319-23093-1_4

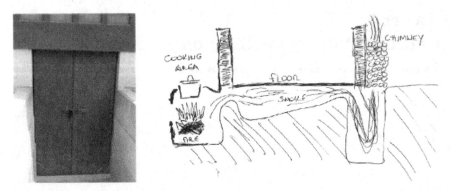

Fig. 4.1 On the *left hand side* the entrance to the ondol is shown. On the *right* a schema of the ondol technology is sketched. The fire on a hearth is used for cooking, the hot smoke is piped under a floor construction and in this way heats the rooms above. The cooled down smoke leaves the building through the chimney on the *right*

combination with instrumental aspects as relevant in the interaction with technology. Technologies supporting both categories of needs are present in a high probability in every home. But in general, they are operated side by side on different infrastructures. Separated in the categories *white goods* and *brown goods* they are typically also operated by different means of interaction.

The societal structures and living circumstances prevalent in the eras of Heron, da Vinci or de Caus are not comparable to those we are typically living in today. Smartness in the illustrated form was merely present in public or religious contexts. If it was available in private areas, then it was reserved for the rich and members of the upper classes and often times required the operation and maintenance by members of lower classes, servants or slaves. The next passages are devoted to the historical developments which can be considered the starting phases of living circumstances that are comparable to those prevalent today.

The modern concept of the home gained relevance after major societal changes. First, the bourgeoisie and later, in the context of the industrial revolution [4], the working class became important parts of society. Societal upheavals were accompanied by new family constellations and the separation of work and life led to new forms of dwelling [5]. In these periods the prototype of the *ideal home* was coined, a detached house with a yard, as described in more detail in Chap. 3. The changes in societies where accompanied by progresses in domestic technology, which became necessary due to changes in demography, urbanisation, and economy. For example, basic needs (warmth, nutrition, light, clothing) could no longer be satisfied by self-production [6]. Whereas rural families in the 1920s still produced 70 % of their own food, urban families could contribute only 2 % to the production of their food [7]. It was necessary to have paid work to afford consumables such as food, firewood and petroleum, to pay rent, and later, to have access to electricity. Because of the need to earn money, the time available for home-based work decreased continually. This resulted in a demand to increase the efficiency of household work, which was one of the drivers for the progress in technology. An indicator for this change is, for example, the stove as a more efficient device that has replaced the kitchen oven [6]. A new era was marked by the introduction of electricity, which, depending on the county and area, dates in the period between 1900 and 1940 [8]. After the profound effects of the second world war, technological progress levelled off resulting in a wider variety of white good appliances such as fridges, electric cookers and washing machines and a differentiation of device categories. At the end of this period the majority of households had access to mains electricity and possessed electrically-powered devices. Interesting effects of the new technologies became salient, such as the fact that, despite the availability of electric appliances, the time spent for household work actually increased. This is because – as a side effect of more efficient devices – demands on cleanliness changed and numbers of cleaning cycles increased [9]. In this way, the new appliances increased output rather than saving time [7].

The category of household devices, brown goods, which fulfilled entertainment needs experienced a diversification. Different forms of radio, television and musical equipment entered the mass market. In the following decades this progress continued. The diversification of home entertainment brought devices supporting the individual use of audio and video content. Tape-based devices enabled an independent and flexible replaying and recording of audio and video for private purposes. Devices like the compact audio cassette were the prevalent technologies when I was a boy. At this time we were happy and satisfied with the things that were possible. In regard to the content quality they were far from the levels that we are used to today. In terms of comfort and ease of use, in some aspects the situation could be considered to have been better than it is today. For example, exchanging content was very easy. When one of your friends had bought a cassette or recorded it himself one did not have to care about whether the cassette would fit in your own player, or if the content was in the correct format to be played or even if this exchange would infringe copyrights. This changed with digitalization. One paradox in this regard has been that the same container could include almost any digital content. I remember when a relative of mine came across a DVD the first time which contained a selection of football games. Having been familiar with digital audio in form of the CD, she was very surprised and asked: *"Who would ever be interested to listen to a football game?"* I think she was probably not the only one who was confused about the mixture of containers and contents, not even to speak about the different recording formats (DVD+, DVD-, DVD-RW, etc.) and regional codes. Taking into consideration the potential problems with interaction caused by inappropriate cues, as pointed out by [10], the *silver disks* in this regard were a regression rather than progress. Today physical containers have all but disappeared and been replaced by virtual containers such as Mp3 and Mp4 which have become the new standard. Meanwhile, the variety of digital formats has led to what is now commonly referred to as the format war. Given the number of combinatorial possibilities, it is not surprising that we are often confronted with error messages such as: *"This file format is not supported by your device"*; *"Codec not found"*; *"This file is not available in your country"*.

In comparison to the reasonable changes in the entertainment sector, changes in the white goods sector are not as spectacular. Devices which have already been on the market for quite a long time, such as vacuum cleaners, washing machines, dishwashers, or cooling devices, have been further developed in regard to their efficiency, but have not experienced many revolutionary developments. Only a few innovative technologies such as microwave ovens, induction cookers or cleaning robots have been introduced.

In the context of almost each technological advance, we can observe that promises have been made; promises that there will not just be progress in a specific segments, but that the devices in the home will grow together into a fully-integrated smart system in the near future [11]. High definition television really followed devices that carried the label *HD-ready*, but this example is one of very few exceptions to the rule: not many of the promises of technological revolutions in the home have come true, specifically in regard to the smart home. As illustrated in Chap. 1, a fully integrated smart home continues to be the exception rather than the rule. This is astonishing because some of the other technologies enumerated above have disseminated quite impressively, speaking of developed countries. For example, major domestic appliances such as washing machines, which have already been on the market for quite a long time have unsurprisingly, attained a penetration of 95 % [12]. In a similar percentage, around 95 % [13, 14] of homes have a TV. Personal computers, which were introduced at about the same time as the smart home, have attained a penetration of 70 % [15]; and the same applies to the significantly younger broadband internet, which is now also available in around 70 % of households [16].

Despite of the problems that have been emphasized in regard to the digital format war, a convergence is observable in some areas of technology. Analogue audio and video contents and physical containers have transformed into virtual container formats, which originated in the realm of computing. The computer as a device was first brought into the home in the form of the PC. Advances in multimedia were first available only locally: examples being improvements in the quality of sound, colour depth, and display resolution. When the Internet came into private households, and when broadband connections followed, extensions such as in-home WLAN networks became of interest for private households. More recently, the spread of mobile devices such as tablets and smart phones was accompanied by the expansion of broadband mobile networks.

All these technological developments could, theoretically, have paved the way for the smart home. Smart technologies should have taken over the part of integration and networking but those integrative features are still missing in an average home. When breaking down the numbers provided by, for example [17–20], the current percentage of penetration of integrated smart systems is in the single-digits. Systems promising to offer *smart* features have entered the market, but the majority of them are still stand-alone devices or cohesive sets of devices which are, at best, difficult to combine or integrate with other smart devices – to say nothing of the integration of conventional devices present in a home. Many of these systems just offer some form of remote control. But as [21] points out, the ability to remotely control a home, even if it is done with a cutting-edge smart phone, does not mean smartness; smartness has to be more.

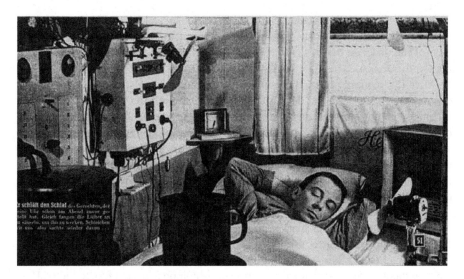

Fig. 4.2 The engineer within his self-established smart home (Taken from [23, p. 13])

To achieve a better understanding of the state-of-the-art the next passages are devoted to the historical developments of technology that can be considered as the direct ancestor of the smart home. According to ([22], p. 75), the smart home was considered a "... *natural extension of current electronic, information and communication technologies*". In the 1960s the first hype, a broader interest in such enhanced functionality can be observed [8]. But even earlier, since around the 1940s [11], related industrial activities can be observed. One example of the technical possibilities of the early days of smart home technology is illustrated in a news article from the 1950s, describing an engineer who developed a self-constructed smart home. The available features included a timer which automatically switched off lights after 10 p.m. and a *toilet occupied* signal [23]. An impression of the system is given in Fig. 4.2. Compared to those available in current smart homes, the possibilities were quite limited.

An important step in home automation was the introduction of computer technology enabling the software based programming of smart home systems. A pioneering work in this regard was the electronic computing home operator (Echo IV) [24]. Computing technology and software programming brought a revolutionary leap in terms of technological possibilities but, as the situation in Fig. 4.2 convey a questionable "*Menschenbild*", putting the focus on the technology and considering the human as an element, that is somewhere in-between. This understanding is obviously still present in the heads of some technicians and developers and one of the central goals of the WISE approach is to change those basic mental models. In this regard, one important example is a product that, according to [25], was not really intended to be a product, but that reflects an understanding of the role and model of technology of the 1960s. This might have been meant sarcastically in the example of the kitchen computer, but is meant seriously and it is present in different forms of advertisement today. The message conveyed to all of us consumers with each of the different devices is that, if we fail in fulfilling our roles, it is never the fault of the device.

After the pioneer phase, the home automation market also experienced some diversification. Over the last decades a separation between automation technologies for industrial and public functional buildings on the one hand and the residential building sector on the other, is observable. In the functional building sector, wired solutions have been successfully adopted. Consider, for example KNX, which enables the integration of components from different manufacturers and offers a high functional range. However, the complexity of system architectures, the pricing and maintenance models have, so far, impeded broad dissemination on the private consumer market.

In the private consumer market, wireless solutions constitute the majority. The following enumeration is consciously not taking into account those smart systems that originate from other sectors, but focusses on *operational technologies*, as [26] labelled them, approaching smartness from basic components and functionality. But even the variety of systems in this segment seems to be incomprehensible.

A simple web search[1] reveals systems from Belkin, Xavax, EQ-3, AVM, RWE, Allnet, D-Link, Coco, Edimax, eSaver, REV, Zipato, Loxone, Somfy, Elro, Brennenstuhl, Taphome, gigaset, BTicino, intertechno[2] and this list is certainly not exhaustive. In the low price segment addressing the end consumer, compatibility and interoperability is typically not present. The strangest example I came across when analysing the market is a manufacturer who has 5 systems on the market. Some of the devices have the same shape, probably have comparable hardware components and seem to operate on the same radio frequency; but they are all branded differently, and they are all incompatible.

There are a few exceptions driven by initiatives and consortia such as Enocean, z-Wave, or Qvivicon, which enable the combined use of devices from different manufacturers. However, the core problem for the consumer is that a decision made in favor of one system and against the others is final. Because of the technical constraints the systems have to deal with, they offer more or less the same principal functions. Technical constraints can be, for example, the wiring standards smart components have to be attached to, and available spaces in households where additional components can be placed. For the average customer it is difficult to find out whether or not a particular system might fulfil ones needs, and whether one system can cover the range of functionality better than the other. Pushing proprietary systems is understandable from an economic perspective, but such a policy could motivate customers to avoid all similar technology instead of adopting one particular brand. In my opinion this has contributed to the current degree of low dissemination of smart home technology (Fig. 4.3).

---

[1] Because the search is started on a computer in Austria, the hits correspond to this market.

[2] All of the brand names serve as examples and are used courtesy of their manufacturers.

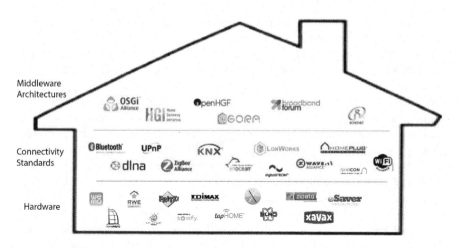

Fig. 4.3 Smart home systems (Adapted from [27])

However, the lack of appropriate interconnecting technology in an average home is only one aspect of the problem. Another aspect which additionally complicates the situation is that those technologies that were successful, such as computing and entertainment electronics – have now developed their own networking and integration facilities. In my opinion, this should have been the responsibility of smart technology. Instead, the number of proprietary and brand-specific infrastructures increases. Standards such as DLNA are present, but not supported by all manufacturers and specifically not available in the low-cost segment. The combination of all of the separate developments and advances, has resulted in a level of complexity on the end consumer market that an average user probably cannot understand. Systems characterized as smart are today offered by global players in the electronic appliance market, focussing on the control of their proprietary appliances (e.g. white goods). Big players coming from ICT are either working on smart home market strategies or already offer their own, mostly proprietary smart home systems, conceptualized surrounding their own key devices: smart phones or tablets. Even car manufacturers meanwhile offer the ability to control technology at home on their in-car systems, though it is, of course, controlled from the perspective of the car. In between these factions one might find the systems I consider to be *"original"* smart home systems. Systems which address smartness from basis of the elementary functions and components enabling the control of lighting, heating, shade, locking, etc.

In general, the different forms of technology present in the home are not integrated. When taking a look at other markets, the automotive sector for example, the situation is different. Most in-car systems are based on integration and the sharing of resources. A state-of-the-art car has integrated around 50 microprocessors and kilometers of cables and is comparable to an average house in terms of technical complexity. The difference is that the integration of the technology is much better than in an average home. This is not a surprise, because cars are compound products and, as a result, it is much easier to configure them so that all of the technology in place is compatible and integrated. This is a pre-requisite due to space limitations and the need to tune and coordinate the flow of energy. However, many manufacturers are producing components for cars and could obviously agree upon standardization.

All the same, as pointed out in Chap. 3, there is some kind of technological standardization in the home, and it could be further pushed in this direction. This would probably also lead to a better utilization of resources, as can be demonstrated again by the example of a car. In a car there is probably only one central display but this conveys different information about all components of the car. For example, information about the technical status, information related to security issues, and also entertainment information (e.g. the current radio station selected) is displayed in the single, general display area. This principle idea of sharing resources probably could have prevented the situation that was described in the birthday story. One of the challenges for a WISE home is therefore to integrate devices present in the home, whether they serve instrumental or entertainment purposes, into one, holistic home system.

As I have tried to illustrate in this chapter, the paradox is that the basic technology is available. We do not have the problem of missing technology, we face the problem of having too much of it. No universal standards are in sight. One could express it with the words of Tanenbaum, a famous computer scientist. *"The nice thing about standards is that you have so many to choose from"*.[3] This quote was clearly intended to be humorous. A potentially serious application of it can be found in the next chapter.

The technology has to assume an integrative role and exploit technical possibilities, such as those based on AI. Consider the example from the birthday story, told earlier. Such situations have to be overcome by the WISE home. This is important, for example, to solve the imminent societal challenges of the triple E (Elderly, Energy and Effectuation) discussed in Chap. 1.

But there could also be other reasons, for example [28–31], refer to the cost aspect (financial as well as effort- and time-related) as a potential hindrance.

References

1. Papadopoulos, E. (2007). Heron of Alexandria (c. 1085 AD). In *Distinguished figures in mechanism and machine science* (pp. 217–245). Dordrecht: Springer.
2. http://www.bl.uk/manuscripts/Viewer.aspx?ref=arundel_ms_263_f001r.
3. Caus, S. D. (1977). *Von gewaltsamen Bewegungen Beschreibung etlicher, sowol nützlichen alls lustigen Machiner.* Hannover: Vincentz.

---

[3]http://en.wikiquote.org/wiki/Andrew_S._Tanenbaum

4. Du Vall, N., & Du, V. N. (1988). *Domestic technology: A chronology of developments* (p. 535). Boston: GK Hall.
5. Moore, J. (2000). Placing home in context. *Journal of Environmental Psychology, 20*(3), 207–217.
6. Cowan, R. S. (1998). How we get our daily bread, or the history of domestic technology revealed. *Magazine of History, 12,* 9–12.
7. Bittman, M., Rice, J. M., & Wajcman, J. (2004). Appliances and their impact: The ownership of domestic technology and time spent on household work. *The British Journal of Sociology, 55*(3), 401–423.
8. Aldrich, F. (2003). Smart homes: Past, present and future. In R. Harper (Ed.), *Inside the smart home* (pp. 17–39). London/New York: Springer.
9. Edwards, W. K., & Grinter, R. E. (2001, January). At home with ubiquitous computing: Seven challenges. In *Ubicomp 2001: Ubiquitous computing* (pp. 256–272). Berlin/Heidelberg: Springer.
10. Norman, D. A. (2002). *The design of everyday things.* New York: Basic books.
11. Mozer, M. (2004). *Lessons from an adaptive house.* Doctoral dissertation, University of Colorado.
12. SMART-A Project (2008). Synergy potential of smart appliances. http://www.smart-a.org/WP2_D_2_3_Synergy_Potential_of_Smart_Appliances.pdf.
13. Plasser, F., & Plasser, G. (2002). *Global political campaigning: A worldwide analysis of campaign professionals and their practices.* Westport: Greenwood Publishing Group.
14. Bride Side of News – Technology Oriented News. http://www.brightsideofnews.com/2011/01/26/digital-divide-global-household-penetration-rates-for-technology/.
15. OECD (2014). Computer, internet and telecommunication. In *OECD Factbook 2013: Economic, environmental and social statistics.* http://www.oecd-ilibrary.org/docserver/download/3013081e.pdf.
16. OECD (2013). Broadband internet penetration. http://www.oecd.org/sti/broadband/broadband-statistics-update.htm.
17. United States Census Bureau. Household statistics. http://quickfacts.census.gov/qfd/states/00000.html.
18. Eurostat. European household composition statistics. http://epp.eurostat.ec.europa.eu/statistics_explained/index.php/Household_composition_statistics.
19. Greenwich Consulting. Smart home – Hope or hype? http://greenwich-consulting.com/sites/greenwich-consulting.com/files/Thoughts-Jan2013_1.pdf.
20. Group Special Mobile Association (GSMA). Smart home report. http://www.gsma.com/connectedliving/wp-content/uploads/2012/03/vision20of20smart20home20report.pdf.
21. Mennicken, S., Vermeulen, J., & Huang, E. M. (2014). From today's augmented houses to tomorrow's smart homes: New directions for home automation research. In *Proceedings of the 2014 ACM International Joint Conference on Pervasive and Ubiquitous Computing,* Seattle (pp. 105–115). ACM.
22. Chan, M., Estève, D., Escriba, C., & Campo, E. (2008). A review of smart homes – Present state and future challenges. *Computer Methods and Programs in Biomedicine, 91*(1), 55–81.
23. Horx, M. (2008). *Technolution: Wie unsere Zukunft sich entwickelt.* Frankfurt: Campus.
24. Spicer, D. (2000). If you can't stand the coding, stay out of the kitchen: Three chapters in the history of home automation. *Doctor Dobb's.* http://www.drdobbs.com/architecture-and-design/if-you-cant-stand-the-coding-stay-out-of/184404040
25. Atkinson, P. (2010). The curious case of the kitchen computer: Products and non-products in design history. *Journal of Design History, 23*(2), 163–179.
26. Augusto, J. C., & McCullagh, P. (2007). Ambient intelligence: Concepts and applications. *Computer Science and Information Systems, 4*(1), 1–27.
27. Bristow, P. (2015). Is it worth waiting for a Universal Standard for the Smart Home? http://cablecongress.com/guest-blog-paul-bristow/.
28. Ding, D., Cooper, R. A., Pasquina, P. F., & Fici-Pasquina, L. (2011). Sensor technology for smart homes. *Maturitas, 69*(2), 131–136.

29. Hindus, D. (1999). The importance of homes in technology research. In *Cooperative buildings. Integrating information, organizations, and architecture* (pp. 199–207). Berlin/Heidelberg: Springer.
30. Sponselee, A. M. A., Schouten, B. A., Bouwhuis, D. G., & Rutten, P. G. S. (2008). Effective use of smart home technology to increase well-being. *Gerontechnology, 7*(2), 211.
31. Yamazaki, T. (2006). Beyond the smart home. In *International Conference on Hybrid Information Technology, 2006 (ICHIT'06)*, Cheju Island (Vol. 2, pp. 350–355). IEEE.

Chapter 5
Theoretical Foundations of the WISE Home

Given the complexity and variety of potentially relevant aspects in the interaction with and within a home in general and a smart home in particular, field-based, longitudinal research is the only chance for appropriately covering the whole scope. This research has to be performed within real world living environments to be able to thoroughly understand *situatedness* [1]; the interplay between characteristics of the home (or better, the house as the surrounding infrastructure), its inhabitants, and the available technology. This form of research has a long-standing scientific tradition in the social sciences and humanities (as will be pointed out in Chap. 6) and has also gained importance in HCI, inspired by respective research activities in CSCW [2].

However, before being able to research technology in the field, specific challenges must be tackled. Given the low dissemination of advanced smart technology, as pointed out in the previous chapters, there is also a low probability of finding facilities that already have integrated such technology that would be required in order to study the triadic relation between house, inhabitants and (smart) technology. In order to make it possible to conduct field research, an alternative strategy would have to be found. Analogously to other approaches in field research, the goal of the attempts to reach the WISE home was therefore to develop prototype systems which could easily be installed and retrofitted. The prototypes have to be flexible and mobile to enable the provision of basic technology to potential users and to be used it in a daily manner under real world conditions. Unlike with single and mobile devices, the difficulty is that smart technology has to be integrated. To succeed at the original experimental design, an unusual amount of additional preparatory work was therefore necessary. In accordance with the theoretical discussion of the last chapters a WISE platform home was established which meets the proposed requirements.

© Springer International Publishing Switzerland 2015
G. Leitner, *The Future Home is Wise, Not Smart*, Computer Supported
Cooperative Work, DOI 10.1007/978-3-319-23093-1_5

5.1   Technical Foundation

An indispensable part of WISE is a technological basis which supports a flexible
and customized implementation of hard- and software components and in this
way enables the thorough investigation of a broad variety of phenomena that
are related to technology in the home. It was emphasised in Chap. 4 that the
majority of smart home systems available on the end consumer market generally
lack compatibility and interoperability. Although there are initiatives and consortia
striving for interoperability and standardization, they were either not available or
not appropriate (because of technical requirements and limitations) when the work
presented in this book was started. The approach followed was therefore to develop
an own system that provides the required flexibility and possibility of customization,
but also takes into account the compatibility and interoperability issues pointed out
in Chap. 4.

Those issues could be addressed with an appropriate architecture which it
is based on software components which enable the integration of devices from
different manufacturers offering, therefore, a wide range of functionality. The
system is based on a service oriented architecture (SOA), which integrates hardware
devices either as providers of a certain service (e.g. visual display) or as service
users. In the concrete realization the WISE platform is implemented on the basis
of an OSGi middleware architecture as a central component. The reason for using
OSGi was that the platform is open both in terms of free of charge use and the
possibility for customization and, in terms of further development and enhancement.
A growing community of developers, researchers and companies contribute to the
development of OSGi. As a result, it can be considered the leading architecture in the
domain of research-oriented smart homes. Numerous research projects following
many different goals are running on OSGi [3–5]. The custom solution to support the
WISE approach was initially build and further developed by [6–8]. The high level
architecture of the platform is laid out in Fig. 5.1. A more detailed description of the
platform is presented in [9] and [10].

The hardware-related layers of the architecture are responsible for the integration
of attached devices and their provision to the system in an abstracted form (labelled
as systems A, B and C to emphasize their different origins). With this abstraction
a user or an external system connected to the platform can handle them as if
they were elements of a single system. The platform was sequentially enhanced;
first installed and tested in the lab facilities of the university, then transferred
to the real world test bed, described in Chap. 7 and related publications such as
[11, 12] and [13]. Finally the platform was deployed in the course of a larger
scale field project, Casa Vecchia,[1] which is also described in more detail in
Chap. 7 and the related publications [9, 14, 15]. Because of its modular nature, the

---

[1]http://www.casavecchia.at, the project was funded by the Austrian Research Promotion Agency
and the Privatstiftung Kärntner Sparkasse in the program line benefit, Project.No. 825889.

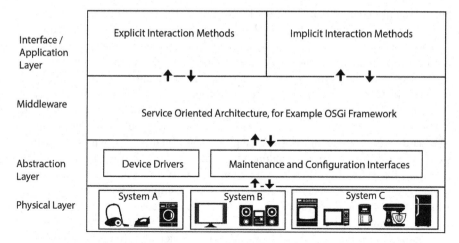

Fig. 5.1 Platform architecture illustrating the integration of devices from different manufacturers (labelled as systems *A*, *B* and *C*) in the base layer, the abstraction and middleware responsible for the provision of services in the middle and the possibilities for accessing devices over these services with explicit and implicit interaction on the top layer

platform supports adaptive and customized integration into different environments and living circumstances and has a functional range that can incorporate features that are typically not available in standard state-of-the-art smart home systems. This includes, for example, health and security functions [15] as well as functions related to energy management [8], entertainment, and comfort [16, 17].

A prerequisite for a software platform to work in the intended way is appropriate hardware which has integrated components that cover the required range of functionality. Investigations were conducted into the availability of smart home systems which would fulfil those requirements. One initial challenge was the inherent difficulty of retrofitting smart technology into real world living environments. After all, the latter are not generally designed and built for the integration of ambient intelligence [18–20]. One important requirement was therefore that a suitable hardware would have to be small enough in size to be integrated even into a very limited amount of space. In order to support interconnection and networking without having to invest high manual efforts, wireless systems were the first choice [9–11]. Another requirement suitable systems had to fulfil was related to costs. In contrast to costs that can occur in research contexts, expenses for the field installations were intended to be within the budget of average private homes – both in terms of initial financial investments and in terms of costs related to the manual efforts for retrofitting and maintenance [21–24]. A final requirement was the potential flexibility that, at that point, could only be estimated on the basis of the features a system already offered. This flexibility should allow the system to be customized in order to suit a broad variety of future requirements that were still, at the time the research attempts described in this book were started, partly unknown; technical requirements such as the possibility to extend the functional range, and, human requirements that had not yet been defined. Even with these constraints, a market survey revealed an almost incomprehensible variety of potentially suitable systems (as illustrated in Chap. 4). As has been pointed out in Chap. 4, systems and devices carrying the label *smart home* are offered through a number of distribution channels with different functional orientations. The final hardware basis (described in detail in Chap. 7) consisted of five subsystems. This was not only the case because no singular system could cover the required functional range. It was also intended as a proof of concept for the flexibility and adaptability of the platform. The hardware covering the biggest range of functionality is a wireless off-the-shelf system from a German manufacturer. The predecessor system served as the hardware basis for the initial development of the WISE platform. It had to be exchanged because of technical limitations, for example, missing bi-directional communication. Another system which could be integrated was a powerline system from Switzerland, which was intended to cover areas in households where wireless communication is impossible or it would not be acceptable because of concerns regarding electronic smog. Custom solutions based on the Arduino® smartboard platform could be integrated supporting the development of custom hardware that provides functionality which was not available in any suitable hardware platform on the market. Finally, it was possible to establish a communication gateway between the WISE platform and another smart home software platform, building brain, which was developed by colleagues from the University of Udine. The focus of building brain is the support of large scale smart environments, such as smart cities. The ability to establish an interface between the two platforms additionally demonstrated the flexibility of our approach.

The integrated hard- and software platform is only a prerequisite for the central goal of the WISE approach – being able to study human computer interaction within the specific context of the home. More concretely, the goal is to be able to study the interaction between users and a smart home system under real world conditions. Two principle forms of interaction with a smart home system could be identified as a result of our own theoretical work and the work of others in the field (as presented in the previous chapters). The first is labelled *explicit interaction*, which [25] called purposeful and direct interaction, and which covers the voluntary and intentional interaction between a user and a smart home system. The second is *implicit interaction* (incidental interaction in [25]'s nomenclature) and is based on the analysis of activity in and interaction with components of the home, for example in the course of rituals and habits. The observation and analysis of such behaviours with AI features can be used to calculate predictions for activities and to derive automatic functions. There are major differences between the WISE platform and state-of-the-art smart home systems. First, standard smart home systems are, in general, not capable of acting smartly in the long term, because they do not have the necessary capabilities, such as a *data or knowledge base* that would make it possible to store data for further analysis. Second, standard smart home systems lack an appropriate algorithmic basis for advanced data analyses, such a *reasoning* and *pattern recognition*, which would make it possible to derive conclusions and to automate functions based on the stored data. Third, the WISE system integrates explicit and implicit interaction features in order to resolve conflicts that result from the different types of intelligences, as has been pointed out in Chap. 2 and [9, 10, 26–28].

5.1.1 Means and Possibilities of Explicit Interaction

The first form of interaction discussed in detail is explicit interaction. As pointed out in Chap. 2 interaction in and with a home has to be observed in a broader sense than in, for example, desktop settings [11, 12, 15, 29, 30]. When considering the interaction between a user and even a conventional home, there are many possibilities for explicit interaction. This could be triggering a wall-mounted switch, a switch on a device itself, or, a button on a remote control. In a smart home, this variety is expanded, because a smart home additionally enables interaction via software interfaces, for example from a desktop computer, a smart phone or a tablet. The result, for a fully-fledged smart home, can be a very high level of complexity. This makes it difficult to define interfaces [31] that appropriately meet user requirements. Figure 5.2 shows examples of possible means of explicit interaction in a smart home. The example is limited to tactile and visual interfaces, but multi-modal interaction, for example with speech and gesture would also be possible.

According to the original understanding of a *smart home*, all devices would have to be integrated into one system to give a user the impression that the home is a holistic entity [32, 33]. This is in clear contrast to the accumulation of stand-alone devices or technology typically present in a home. State-of-the-art technologies are based on an incomprehensibly vast and varied range of distinct interaction

Fig. 5.2 Different forms of interfaces in a smart home and devices that can be controlled by them

principles, leading to an exacerbation of *remote control anarchy* [34]. To overcome the potentially related problems the WISE approach reconsiders basic concepts of human computer interaction and applies them to the context of the home. One of those concepts is the characteristics of interaction introduced by [35], which are, for example, affordances (or their new name – signifiers – [36]), feedback, mapping or constraints. To emphasize their relevance the characteristics of a smart switch are investigated. A smart switch can be considered to represent an *internet of things* (IoT) device [37]. It constitutes a hybrid device that has the look and feel of a conventional wall-mounted switch but is independent from wiring and other physical constraints. The functions that can be triggered by such a switch can be located anywhere and therefore do not cause a feedback in the location the switch itself is located. This can affect the comprehension of mapping (where are the devices located that are triggered by the switch) as well as feedback mechanisms (in what status are the triggered devices). Appropriately considering the accompanying circumstances to avoid pitfalls of incomprehensible functionality, as described by [38, 39] is a central requirement of WISE interaction. Components would have to provide appropriate features to support the mental models of the users. In regards to a smart switch, the mental model of a user is probably more similar to a conventional wall mount switch rather than a remote control (although they might be the same from the technical point of view, as illustrated in Fig. 5.3). The relevance of this difference will be illustrated in Chap. 7.

Specifically in the context of the home, and because of attentional and motivational aspects (which were addressed in Chap. 2) it is important to ensure an easy, intuitive interaction with a smart home system. In this regard, current movements in HCI question the concepts of *user*, *task* and point out coming changes, such as the *end of interface stability* [29]. Appropriate technology should be designed in a way that would enable users to freely choose which devices to use for interaction, and in what order and combination to use them; selecting the appropriate means and modality with which to perform any given interaction. This freedom of choice occurs naturally in human to human interaction, where the combination

Fig. 5.3 Remote control and wall switch of a smart home system, representing two different designs of one and the same technical component

Table 5.1 The table illustrates the differences and commonalities of the WISE concept and URC

Wise	URC
Application Layer	Controllers
Middleware Layer	UI Protocol Layer
	UI Socket Layer
Bridge Layer	Target Adapter Layer
Hardware Layer	Target

and the change between gesture, tactile, and verbal interaction works smoothly. In contrast to this experience, devices and systems present in current homes are typically concentrated on brand- and manufacturer-specific concepts, which are often incomprehensible for the user, specifically when they have to be used in a combined way. A way to overcome these problems and increase the ease of interaction with technology in the home would some kind of convention which is also found in human to human interaction. Conventions determine what form of interaction is appropriate and what is not. This approach could be used to enhance explicit interaction.

One concept to support such conventions is URC (Universal Remote Console) [40]. The universal remote console strives for a standardization of interfaces to the hardware layers and enables a *seamless* access to the devices integrated in a system (such as a smart home system) from a broad variety of software interfaces. As illustrated in Table 5.1, URC has some parallels to the lower layers of the WISE platform because it is also based on the abstraction of devices in order to make them accessible on standardized protocols or, as it was termed above, conventions.

URC has its focus more on the hardware and back-end software rather than on the interface level. It addresses basic problems of the integration of devices, and so has parallels to the WISE approach. The history of software interfaces has shown that high degrees of freedom in the design do not always have a positive effect. Such a negative development of interfaces in terms of usability is observable in myriad mobile device apps, and has meanwhile reached the smart home field. One could have an app for the refrigerator to check its contents, another app for the kitchen oven to upload recipes for automated cooking, and yet another app to start the washing machine remotely. These apps are typically based on corporate design and brand strategies rather than on standard interaction concepts.

In this regard, the definition of conventions would also make sense. One promising concept to achieve this goal is User Interface or HCI patterns [41]. These patterns were introduced by Alexander who described principle solutions for recurring problems in architectural contexts [42]. The benefits of patterns is their ability to abstract concrete problems to their principle elements. A well-known pattern for interface design is, for example, the shopping cart in online shopping platforms. Although the cart can be quite different in terms of design, location in the website and basic elements (e.g. the available payment possibilities) the principle steps (put items into the cart, change/remove items, check payment and shipping options, finish the process and checkout) are the same. By taking into account such patterns a WISE home would help to solve the problems related to inconsistencies and incomprehensible procedures. For example, the problems related to the VCR clock example presented in Chap. 1.

Most people in the western world have to deal with the problem of resetting their clocks twice a year, when the time has to be changed from winter to summertime or vice versa. It is fascinating to consider the many different ways in which one might set a clock. With appropriate patterns such tasks could be made more intuitive for their users. This is true for generally simple things as clock setting, but also for more complex tasks such as programming procedures (on a VCR, DVD Recorder, Harddisk Recorder, Mp3-Device or NAS), and for procedures that only occur infrequently – such as the decalcification of a coffee maker. All of the mentioned examples are probably that difficult to use, because the focus in their design was on the availability of technical components instead of the tasks, capabilities or experiences of their users.

In the home context the application of patterns need not be limited to virtual interfaces like the shopping cart. Pattern could be applied beyond virtual interfaces and across virtual and hardware interfaces present in the home. On the example of the many different forms of heating controls that are present in the home [15] the respective possibilities are emphasised. On a radiator, there is typically a circular knob to control temperature, and the same applies for room thermostats. But when observing smart home control software, temperature controls are often represented as sliders. Sliders are standard widgets in GUI design and this is probably why they are used for the design of temperature controls on virtual interfaces. The physical knob, however, has a better affordance and is more intuitive to a user. Additionally, its form factor is dependent on the physical constraints of the radiator valve (which is circular). Patterns would have to take into consideration all those aspects and, in the best case, the result would be a collection of standardized, intuitive, multi-modal and cross-platform applicable interaction patterns, that fulfil the requirement that are best described with: *"Don't make me think"* [43].

Concepts such as URC or Interface patterns could help to overcome several problems that occur in the home; problems which can currently be solved by smart technology, but not in a WISE way. For example, I assume that everyone knows the situation either personally or second-hand, when a TV is still working but the remote control is broken. Specifically for outdated televisions, it is often impossible to get an original spare remote, or it is too expensive and not worth a high investment. The solution is often a universal remote control. Most of the time these controllers are completely different from the original, in terms of look, feel, and handling. Elderly people in particular therefore shy away from changing their remote until it is completely broken. If an exchange cannot be delayed, do-it-yourself solutions to prevent elderly or inexperienced users from pressing the wrong buttons have to be applied. Examples for that can be found on several internet fora, for example.[2]

If remote controls were based more on standardized patterns and interaction conventions, rather than on brand-specific interaction concepts, this would be a step in the right direction and would not make necessary the work-arounds mentioned.

Another development on the level of software interfaces that could support the demand for a higher intuitiveness and more understandable interaction is HTML 5. Whereas interface patterns are focused on the basic building blocks of interaction, HTML 5 provides means for an appropriate implementation and design of the interface. This is possible because HMTL 5 can help to overcome inconsistencies, limitations and specifications of platforms, such as iOS, Android or Windows.

An important addition to HTML 5 to achieve the goal of enhanced interaction is the concept of responsive design [44] which illustrates possibilities to develop interfaces in a platform-independent and consistent way. The central idea of responsive design is that a developer of an interface never knows who the users of his system might be, and, more importantly, what device a user is currently using to interact with the system. The uncertainty of not knowing what devices a user is taking for interaction as well as the need to provide an optimal experience also applies to the smart home. PC, smartphone and tablets are only a few examples of the variety of tools with which a user could interact with a smart home system. The cumbersome solution would be to implement an interface for every platform separately to ensure that every user would have an optimal experience. Responsive design is based on the second alternative. With concepts such as cascading stylesheets and media queries responsive design supports an enhanced level of usability on different devices and platforms.

Taking into account conventions does not have to result in a mishmash of boring and similar-looking interfaces. I would like to use again an example from the automotive sector at this point. Most people would probably agree that the diversity of cars is broad, especially in terms of design. Despite this diversity, each car can be controlled on the basis of more or less standardized patterns. Most cars have a steering wheel, an assembly of pedals, a gear box. These basic elements and conventions that define their design and position in a car ensure that people can drive every car, in principle, even if it was of a brand a driver has never used before. The conventions do not have to interfere with design, because they still leave appropriate degrees of freedom for the design of cars. Those conventions would therefore also be an appropriate approach to increase the quality of interfaces for the home. It would enable interaction on the basis of generalizable principles and patterns but without limiting the creativity of the design of the interfaces and the platforms that are available.

---

[2]http://areuxperienced.me/2015/05/15/ux-iota-lifes-short-the-crappy-ux-of-most-of-the-things-you-use-daily-make-it-shorter/, http://i.imgur.com/YMbGp3W.jpg, https://www.pinterest.com/pin/425238389786992973/

Taking into account these aspects opens new possibilities, such as to enable users to develop their own applications and interfaces. End user development (EUD, [45]) is, according to [46] the future of human computer interaction. They expect an evolution from systems that are *easy to use* towards systems that are *easy to develop*. However, the change from using basic functionality and interfaces to developing or modifying them requires either an expertise in programming or alternative forms of programming to allow users to build their own programs without requiring such skills. One solution is, for example, visual programming on the basis of basic elements (primitives), as demonstrated by [47]. Such programming alternatives were also investigated in the course of our own work and are presented in Chap. 7.

There are many reasons why EUD will gain importance in the future. One of them is that the need for EUD will increase due to the shift in the population pyramid, according to which the availability of qualified personnel will decrease [48]. Another argument is that, in terms of cycles and flexibility, conventional software development cannot support the variety of needs that would be required in the home context [46]. A third argument, which, in the context of increasing data abuse is probably the most important reason to support EUD, is the consideration of values, such as privacy, independence and autonomy. By giving users the possibility to take and keep control of their own data related threats and fears can be reduced. In [49] and [50], examples are provided showing how end user programming is (and could be) supported by the WISE platform on both a theoretical and a practical level.

The final, but not least important form of explicit interaction that can be considered specifically promising in the context of home is *peripheral*, or *calm* interaction as [51] labelled it. As has been emphasized in the previous chapters, activities in the home are different to those taking place in the workplace. They are often performed in parallel to one another, many of them even not in the focus of attention. However, the electronic devices in general and computerized devices in particular demand focused interaction of their users, as is observable with both mobile devices [52] and with devices in the home [51, 53]. In times of information overload it would specifically make sense to provide alternatives; supporting human capabilities such as peripheral attention or speech and gesture control to communicate with the environment [15]. The WISE platform supports this form of interaction – as is demonstrated, for example, with the design of the central interface of the platform, and alarm and information features available for smart phones, both described in detail in Chap. 7 and [9]. Conveying information on a peripheral level is also possible with pieces of furniture, as illustrated in [8] and [15]. Other forms of peripheral interaction have been conceptualized [54] and evaluated experimentally [55] for gesture and speech interaction, enabling a sort of *laid-back* interaction, as observable in Fig. 7.5, in which a study participant is totally relaxed while interacting with a smart home system. The interfaces in the WISE home platform are designed with a focus on an enhanced level of user experience by using alternative interface concepts such as informative art [56, 57].

5.1.2 Means and Possibilities of Implicit Interaction

The next category of interaction, *implicit interaction* is also happening peripherally, but with the difference to peripheral interaction that it is not requiring explicit triggers from users. To identify a need for a change to the system, AI is used. AI constitutes an appropriate basis for smartness, but according to [58] its relevance in ambient intelligence systems is still too low. Specifically in the segment of affordable systems, the provision of customized AI features fails in terms of appropriate infrastructures (such as databases or advanced analysis features) but also in terms of costs which would be required for their implementation. The WISE platform overcomes these limitations by using the open OSGi architecture which enables the integration of devices from different manufactures (as illustrated in Fig. 5.1), and implements AI features on an abstract, device-independent level. With this approach, enhanced levels of smartness are possible, even on the basis of low-price smart home components or systems. Smartness realized with AI is, for example, able to analyse activity that takes place in the home as *implicit interaction* and derives automated functionality from this activity without the need for the user to explicitly triggering a function. An example for that could be that the system observes that a user is frequently getting up at night and moves from the bedroom to the bathroom. On the basis of data analysis the system could provide a light corridor when this situation happens the next time. This kind of functionality would support a requirement of [25] who demands that a system "... *should get on with its job with little or no communication with the human*". There are different levels of smartness, which are imaginable. Figure 5.4 shows a conceptual model including different levels of smartness which served as a basis in the conceptualization of the enhanced smartness features for the WISE platform.

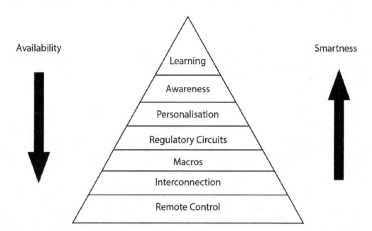

Fig. 5.4 Stages of evolution of smartness in the home starting with remote control on the basic level, followed by the possibility of networking and macro programming and representing personalization, awareness and learning as the highest levels of smartness [10]

When the model depicted in Fig. 5.4 (which is described in detail in [10]) was established we considered the possibility of remote control as an early stage and prerequisite of smartness. This stage does not, according to [59], provide real smartness, because it is just an alternative form of control that requires explicit interaction. The next stage, which already has some form of smartness, is the possibility of networking devices which would enable combined programming (e.g. in the form of macros). The following stage is self-regulatory circuits, on the basis of which automated responses to recurring events can be generated. The stages of highest smartness are personalization, awareness and learning and in this regard similar to the model of [33]. Only these latter stages would support the derivation of real smart functionality. The initial step to achieve them is the analysis of stored historical data to identify regularities and significant deviations. Regularities can be used to automatically trigger functions, deviations could be used to trigger alerts. When the model depicted in Fig. 5.4 was developed, we considered regularities as a specific form of implicit interaction and labelled them *ritual based interaction* [10]. Rituals could serve as a basis for the derivation of automated functions as an alternative to explicit pre-programming of complex functionality such as scenarios. These kind of goal would have a high correlation to wisdom, because one central characteristic, or as [60] puts it *the heart of wisdom*, is tacit, informal knowledge [60, 61, p. 157]; a form of knowledge that is currently under-represented in smart home systems – especially outside of academic research.

Examples of features based on implicit interaction in the form of pattern recognition and pattern matching algorithms have been implemented by [62] and as well as in the part of our own work presented in Chap. 7 and [9]. Recommender and configurator technologies are one area of AI that have been applied in different forms in our work to enhance the quality of interaction with a smart home [63, 64]. Another area of application is multi-user scenarios which have been studied in the context of the real world test bed based on the WISE platform described in detail in Sect. 6.1.2 and [13].

5.1.3   An Integrated Interaction Model

The essential advantage differentiating the WISE home from a *smart* home is that explicit and implicit interaction are smoothly integrated in one system. Recommender and configurator technologies, described for example in [26, 27] and [28] play a central role in this regard. These instantiations of AI technologies are responsible for the pre-processing of complex data, combined with dialogue features to enable the user to communicate decisions and preferences to the system [65]. It is important to ensure that AI and automated features do not overrule the user, as was pointed out as a potential danger in Chap. 2 when different forms of conflicting intelligences meet in the home. The alternative is to enter into a dialogue; proposing or recommending alternatives, and negotiating the best solution. Possibilities of how different forms of recommender systems could be integrated to assist in a variety of tasks in a home are discussed in more detail in the Chap. 7, and are also described in [26]. An example of the implementation of a recommender system enhancing the access to news services by reducing the contents based on historical interests is given in [9]. Possibilities of adapting technical systems in an advanced manner to human capabilities are discussed in [11, 27] and [28]. Persuasive technologies, as one example, can help to compensate de-skilling and demotivation problems that are often associated with the introduction of technology. In the sense of [66], who demands *smart people* instead of *smart homes*, users can be motivated (or persuaded) to actively change their behaviour, for example, to save energy or to engage in mental and physical activities [66]. Technology that requires and supports human effort appropriately can help to keep people mentally and physically healthy [66]. In combination with configuration technology providing adequate interfaces to the users – as discussed in detail in [50] – this constitutes an optimal basis for a WISE behaviour of the system. The combination of HI (human intelligence) and AI helps to avoid problems that occur with conventional smart technology, in which automated procedures sometimes overrule the users [67, 68]. It is not that the technology itself should take over intelligent capabilities of the human; smartness emerges from the smooth interaction between the system and the users [69]. This also means that a system has to be able to act beyond immediate problems (e.g. by considering historical data) and to apply implicit (tacit) knowledge, converging ubiquitous computing and user-friendly interfaces [70], and ensuring that the level of automation is not so high as to give people the impression of being dominated by technology [68, 70] or of being haunted [23].

A model of how explicit and implicit interaction are smoothly integrated, and how tasks could be distributed between the technical system and the user is presented in Fig. 5.5.

Figure 5.5 encompasses the two forms of interaction, *explicit* and *implicit interaction*. Implicit interaction works bottom up and can cover the control and automation of basic infrastructural components available in a home. The lowest layer (building components) includes, for example, wiring and piping, and heating components. Based on past behaviour it would be quite easy for an AI-enhanced system to learn preferences in terms of temperature and apply them considering the delay times of the heating. It is clear that such systems would not currently be able to deal with multiple users. Not yet, but the WISE platform provides a basis to build upon. The next category (installation components) includes electrical sockets or switches. These can also be accessed by automated functions, such as separating sockets from mains power when it is most probable that nobody is in the room any more. However, it is necessary that human users always have the possibility to overrule automatisms. Built-in devices, representing the next layer, include water boilers and stoves, for example. Attached devices are dishwashers, refrigerators, freezers, coffeemakers, TVs, and hifi equipment. With an increasing variety of devices on the market, the variety in the combination of explicit and implicit interactions has also increased. The final group (networked devices) includes computers, printers, smart phones, and tablets. With these devices automated functions have to be applied cautiously. It could, for example, be in the interest

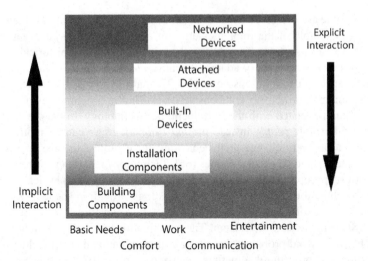

Fig. 5.5 Integrated interaction model based on the model put forward by [19], emphasizing the interplay between implicit and explicit interaction. Implicit interaction works bottom-up and focuses on basic components that are integrated in a household (such as wiring, switches, sockets, household appliances). Explicit interaction works top-down, with a focus on complex, integrated devices such as smart phones, tablets, and computers – but also enables the control of devices of lower layers of the system. Devices of the lower layers of the model support the fulfilment of basic needs and comfort (e.g. warmth, nutrition, hygiene), whereas devices in the upper layers support work (e.g. household work or office work), communication (e.g. phone, e-mail, social networks), and entertainment (e.g. music, video, gaming, TV)

of users to automatically mute or redirect phone calls when a person is most likely to be taking a rest. The borders between the device categories are fluid, because conventional appliances meanwhile have also the possibility of being networked. However, devices in the lower categories are well-suited to the application of automatic procedures based on AI, such as those derived from the analysis of user behaviour. The higher the complexity and functional range of a device or a subsystem (symbolized by a higher category), the more probable it is that people will prefer to interact explicitly. Explicit interaction works top-down and has a higher priority than implicit interaction, which means that it is always possible for a user to access and change the state of any device and subsystem present in the home.

The final goal is that, in the future, the integration of all the devices present in the home and the technologies behind them works as in a car, where automated technologies and explicit user interaction are smoothly integrated. Just think about what happens if a driver pushes the brake pedal. It is in the responsibility of the driver to decide when to push the brake, but the ABS system and stability programs in the backend enhance the efficiency and effectiveness of the brake procedure. The difference is, that, in general, cars are not designed to be technically customized by their users after the purchase. This is somewhat understandable. This is somewhat understandable, but it would be also beneficial for people to have the option to shape the environment, as long as security and safety are not affected. There might be, for example, areas in the home, specifically in regard to entertainment where it would make sense to enable users to adapt functionality by themselves. My understanding of WISE is not to imitate or even supersede the human. What I want to emphasise is that a broader view of HCI in the sense of a *MABA MABA* (man are better at, machines are better at) approach [71]. Each part should concentrate on the abilities and capabilities that it is best for. As it has been displayed in the history of computing, computers are very good at storing information, at processing complex data, at scanning big and complex amounts of information, and at doing repetitive tasks, but they do not have an idea of what could constitute a *good life*.

References

1. Harrison, S., Tatar, D., & Sengers, P. (2007). The three paradigms of HCI. In *Alt. Chi. Session at the SIGCHI Conference on Human Factors in Computing Systems*, San Jose (pp. 1–18).
2. Bannon, L. (2011). Reimagining HCI: Toward a more human-centered perspective. *Interactions, 18*(4), 50–57.
3. Helal, S., Mann, W., El-Zabadani, H., King, J., Kaddoura, Y., & Jansen, E. (2005). The gator tech smart house: A programmable pervasive space. *Computer, 38*(3), 50–60.
4. Gu, T., Pung, H. K., & Zhang, D. Q. (2005). A service-oriented middleware for building context-aware services. *Journal of Network and Computer Applications, 28*(1), 1–18.
5. Ricquebourg, V., Menga, D., Durand, D., Marhic, B., Delahoche, L., & Loge, C. (2006). The smart home concept: Our immediate future. In *1st IEEE International Conference on E-Learning in Industrial Electronics*, Hammamet (pp. 23–28). IEEE.
6. Felsing, D. (2009) *Eine erweiterbare Smart Home Plattform auf Basis des FS20 Systems*. Diploma Thesis, Alpen-Adria Universität Klagenfurt, Klagenfurt.
7. Rabl, W. (2009). *Multimodale Interaktion im Smart-Home-Bereich*. Diploma Thesis, Alpen-Adria Universität Klagenfurt.
8. Fercher, A., Hitz, M., & Leitner, G. (2009). Pervasive approaches to awareness of energy consumption. In *Ami-Blocks*, Salzburg (pp. 3–8). Erlangen, Germany.
9. Leitner, G., Felfernig, A., Fercher, A. J., & Hitz, M. (2014). Disseminating ambient assisted living in rural areas. *Sensors, Special Issue Ambient Assisted Living, 14*(8), 13496–13531.
10. Leitner, G., Melcher, R., & Hitz, M. (2012). Spielregeln im intelligenten Wohnumfeld. In *Vernetzung als soziales und technisches Paradigma* (pp. 189–206). Wiesbaden: Springer.
11. Leitner, G., Hitz, M., & Ahlström, D. (2007). Applicability and usability of off-the-shelf smart appliances in tele-care. In *21st International Conference on Advanced Information Networking and Applications Workshops, 2007 (AINAW'07)*, Niagara Falls (Vol. 2, pp. 881–886). IEEE.
12. Leitner, G., & Fercher, A. J. (2010). AAL 4 ALL – A matter of user experience. In *Aging friendly technology for health and independence* (pp. 195–202). Berlin/Heidelberg: Springer.
13. Ayuningtyas C. *Activity modeling for multi-user environments*. Ph.D. Thesis. Erasmus Mundus Doctorate Program in Interactive and Cognitive Environments (ICE), Alpen Adria Universität Klagenfurt. Work in progress.
14. Leitner, G., Fercher, A. J., Felfernig, A., & Hitz, M. (2012). Reducing the entry threshold of AAL systems: Preliminary results from Casa Vecchia. In *Computers helping people with special needs* (LNCS 7382, pp. 709–715). Berlin/Heidelberg: Springer.
15. Leitner, G., Hitz, M., Fercher, A. J., & Brown, J. N. (2013). Aspekte der human computer interaction im smart home. *HMD Praxis der Wirtschaftsinformatik, 50*(6), 37–47.
16. Chan, M., Estéve, D., Escriba, C., & Campo, E. (2008). A review of smart homes – Present state and future challenges. *Computer Methods and Programs in Biomedicine, 91*(1), 55–81.

17. Balta-Ozkan, N., Boteler, B., & Amerighi, O. (2014). European smart home market development: Public views on technical and economic aspects across the United Kingdom, Germany and Italy. *Energy Research and Social Science, 3*, 65–77.
18. Hindus, D. (1999). The importance of homes in technology research. In *Cooperative buildings. Integrating information, organizations, and architecture* (pp. 199–207). Berlin/Heidelberg: Springer.
19. Barlow, J., & Gann, D. (1998). A changing sense of place: Are integrated it systems reshaping the home? http://139.184.32.141/Units/spru/publications/imprint/sewps/sewp18/sewp18.pdf.
20. Edwards, W. K., & Grinter, R. E. (2001). At home with ubiquitous computing: Seven challenges. In *Ubicomp: Ubiquitous computing* (pp. 256–272). Berlin/Heidelberg: Springer.
21. Dewsbury, G. (2001). The social and psychological aspects of smart home technology within the care sector. *New Technology in the Human Services, 14*(1/2), 9–17.
22. Ding, D., Cooper, R. A., Pasquina, P. F., & Fici-Pasquina, L. (2011). Sensor technology for smart homes. *Maturitas, 69*(2), 131–136.
23. Eckl, R., & MacWilliams, A. (2009). Smart home challenges and approaches to solve them: A practical industrial perspective. In *Intelligent interactive assistance and mobile multimedia computing* (pp. 119–130). Berlin/Heidelberg: Springer.
24. Yamazaki, T. (2006). Beyond the smart home. In *International Conference on Hybrid Information Technology, 2006 (ICHIT'06)*, Cheju Island (Vol. 2, pp. 350–355). IEEE.
25. Dix, A. (2002). Beyond intention-pushing boundaries with incidental interaction. In *Proceedings of Building Bridges: Interdisciplinary Context-Sensitive Computing, Glasgow University*, Glasgow (Vol. 9, pp. 1–6).
26. Leitner, G., Ferrara, F., Felfernig, A., & Tasso, C. (2011). Decision support in the smart home. In *RecSys Workshop on Human Decision Making in Recommender Systems* (pp. 8–16). New York: ACM.
27. Felfernig, A., Gula, B., Leitner, G., Maier, M., Melcher, R., & Teppan, E. (2008). Persuasion in knowledge-based recommendation. In *Persuasive technology* (pp. 71–82). Berlin/Heidelberg: Springer.
28. Felfernig, A., Friedrich, G., Gula, B., Hitz, M., Kruggel, T., Leitner, G., Melcher, R., Riepan, D., Strauss, S., Teppan, E., & Vitouch, O. (2007). Persuasive recommendation: Serial position effects in knowledge-based recommender systems. In *Persuasive technology* (pp. 283–294). Berlin/Heidelberg: Springer.
29. Harper, R. H. (2008). Being human: Human-computer interaction in the year 2020. Cambridge: Microsoft Research Limited.
30. Leitner, G., Ahlström, D., & Hitz, M. (2007). Usability – Key factor of future smart home systems. In *Home informatics and telematics: ICT for the next billion* (pp. 269–278). New York: Springer.
31. Ringbauer, B., Heidmann, D. F., & Biesterfeldt, J. (2003). When a house controls its master. Universal design for smart living environments. In *Proceedings of 10th International Conference on Human-Computer Interaction*, Crete.
32. Alam, M. R., Reaz, M. B. I., & Ali, M. A. M. (2012). A review of smart homes – Past, present, and future. *IEEE Transactions on Systems, Man, and Cybernetics, Part C: Applications and Reviews, 42*(6), 1190–1203.
33. Aldrich, F. (2003). Smart homes: Past, present and future. In R. Harper (Ed.), *Inside the smart home* (pp. 17–39). Berlin/Heidelberg: Springer.
34. Nielsen, J. (2004). Remote control anarchy. Jakob Nielsens Alertbox.
35. Norman, D. A. (1988). *The psychology of everyday things*. New York: Basic books.
36. Norman, D. A. (2010). *Living with complexity*. Cambridge: MIT.
37. Atzori, L., Iera, A., & Morabito, G. (2010). The internet of things: A survey. *Computer Networks, 54*(15), 2787–2805.
38. Dourish, P. (2004). *Where the action is: The foundations of embodied interaction*. Cambridge: MIT.
39. Raskin, J. (2000). *The humane interface: New directions for designing interactive systems*. Reading: Addison-Wesley Professional.

40. Zimmermann, G., Vanderheiden, G., & Gilman, A. (2003). Universal remote console-prototyping for the alternate interface access standard. In *Universal access theoretical perspectives, practice, and experience* (pp. 524–531). Berlin/Heidelberg: Springer.

41. VanWelie, M., & Van der Veer, G. C. (2003). Pattern languages in interaction design: Structure and organization. In *INTERACT 2003 – Ninth IFIP TC13 International Conference on Human-Computer Interaction*, Zurich, 1–5 Sept 2003 (Vol. 3, pp. 1–5).

42. Alexander, C., Ishikawa, S., Silverstein, M., Jacobson, M., Fiksdahl-King, I., & Angel, S. (1977). *A pattern language: Towns, buildings, construction* (Center for environmental structure). New York: Oxford University Press.

43. Krug, S. (2005). *Don't make me think: A common sense approach to web usability.* Berkeley, CA, USA: New Riders Publishers

44. Marcotte, E. (2011). *Responsive web design.* Paris: Editions Eyrolles.

45. Davidoff, S., Lee, M. K., Yiu, C., Zimmerman, J., & Dey, A. K. (2006). Principles of smart home control. In *UbiComp: Ubiquitous computing* (pp. 19–34). Berlin/Heidelberg: Springer.

46. Lieberman, H., Paternó, F., Klann, M., & Wulf, V. (2006). *End-user development: An emerging paradigm* (pp. 1–8). Amsterdam: Springer.

47. Ash, J., Babes, M., Cohen, G., Jalal, S., Lichtenberg, S., Littman, M., & Zhang, E. (2011). Scratchable devices: User-friendly programming for household appliances. In *Human-computer interaction. Towards mobile and intelligent interaction environments* (pp. 137–146). Berlin/Heidelberg: Springer.

48. Pohl, C. (2009). Der Arbeitsmarkt für Pflege im Spiegel demographischer Veränderungen. VKAD infoDienst, 10, 2009.

49. Leitner, G., Fercher, A. J., & Lassen, C. (2013). End users programming smart homes – A case study on scenario programming. In *Human-computer interaction and knowledge discovery in complex, unstructured, big data* (pp. 217–236). Berlin/Heidelberg: Springer.

50. Leitner, G., Felfernig, A., Blazek, P., Reinfrank, F., & Ninaus, G. (2014). *User interfaces for configuration environments, knowledge-based configuration: From research to business cases* (pp. 89–106). Amsterdam: Elsevier.

51. Weiser, M., & Brown, J. S. (1997). The coming age of calm technology. In *Beyond calculation* (pp. 75–85). New York: Springer.

52. Ling, R. (2004). *The mobile connection: The cell phone's impact on society.* Burlington: Morgan Kaufmann.

53. Harper, R. (Ed.). (2011). *The connected home: The future of domestic life.* London: Springer.

54. Brown, J. N. A., Leitner, G., Hitz, M., & Català Mallofré, A. (2014). A model of calm HCI. In *CHI Workshop*, Toronto (pp. 9–12).

55. Brown, J. N. A. (2014). *Unifying interaction across distributed controls in a smart environment using anthropology-based computing to make human-computer interaction "Calm".* Ph.D. Thesis, Erasmus Mundus Doctorate Program in Interactive and Cognitive Environments (ICE), Alpen Adria Universität Klagenfurt, Austria.

56. Redström, J., Skog, T., & Hallnäs, L. (2000). Informative art: Using amplified artworks as information displays. In *Proceedings of DARE 2000 on Designing Augmented Reality Environments*, Ellsinore (pp. 103–114). ACM.

57. Ferscha, A. (2007). A matter of taste. In *Ambient intelligence* (pp. 287–304). Berlin/Heidelberg: Springer.

58. Ramos, C., Augusto, J. C., & Shapiro, D. (2008). Ambient intelligence: The next step for artificial intelligence. *IEEE Intelligent Systems, 23*(2), 15–18.

59. Mennicken, S., Vermeulen, J., & Huang, E. M. (2014). From today's augmented houses to tomorrow's smart homes: New directions for home automation research. In *Proceedings of the 2014 ACM International Joint Conference on Pervasive and Ubiquitous Computing*, Seattle (pp. 105–115). ACM.

60. Sternberg, R. J. (2004). What is wisdom and how can we develop it? *The Annals of the American Academy of Political and Social Science, 591*(1), 164–174.

61. Marcus, A. (2002). Dare we define user-interface design? *Interactions, 9*(5), 19–24.

62. Cook, D. J. (2012). How smart is your home? *Science (New York, NY), 335*(6076), 1579.

63. Jannach, D., Zanker, M., Felfernig, A., & Friedrich, G. (2010). *Recommender systems: An introduction*. New York: Cambridge University Press.
64. Felfernig, A., Hotz, L., Bagley, C., & Tiihonen, J. (2014). *Knowledge-based configuration: From research to business cases*. Newnes. Morgan Kaufmann Publishers (imprint of Elsevier), Amsterdam.
65. Felfernig, A., Schippel, S., Leitner, G., Reinfrank, F., Mandl, M., Blazek, P., Ninaus, G., & Teppan, E. (2013). Automated repair of scoring rules in constraint-based recommender systems. *AI Communications, 26*(1), 15–27.
66. Intille, S. S. (2002). Designing a home of the future. *IEEE Pervasive Computing, 1*(2), 76–82.
67. Randall, D., Harper, R., & Rouncefield, M. (2007). *Fieldwork for design: Theory and practice*. London: Springer.
68. Hamill, L. (2006). Controlling smart devices in the home. *The Information Society, 22*(4), 241–249.
69. Taylor, A. S., Harper, R., Swan, L., Izadi, S., Sellen, A., & Perry, M. (2007). Homes that make us smart. *Personal and Ubiquitous Computing, 11*(5), 383–393.
70. Friedewald, M., Costa, O. D., Punie, Y., Alahuhta, P., & Heinonen, S. (2005). Perspectives of ambient intelligence in the home environment. *Telematics and Informatics, 22*(3), 221–238.
71. Dekker, S. W., & Woods, D. D. (2002). MABA-MABA or abracadabra? Progress on human-automation co-ordination. *Cognition, Technology & Work, 4*(4), 240–244.

Chapter 6
Empirical Foundation of WISE

One of the reasons that the adoption of smart technology is behind forecasted level is the focus on technology emphasized in the previous chapters. This theoretical orientation is questionable, but so are the methodological paths that were followed. I consider the latter as an effect of the former. The constraint focus in smart home research and the lack of consideration for the non-technical aspects [1] have had the follow-up effect that a reasonable amount of empirical work has also been limited in this way. A reasonable proportion of related research is carried out under artificial circumstances in lab facilities or research institutions. As pointed out in Chap. 3, it is easier to investigate the technical layer separated from the other layers of the home, but then sight of the whole is lost. The resulting developments often cover only a fraction of the requirements they should cover. Consider that the prototypes and finished systems are developed and evaluated under artificial conditions that when they are introduced to the real world, they probably appear to be incomplete and unsuitable. The evaluations performed on them in artificial environments are characterized by a low external validity. This seems to be not only a phenomenon in smart home research, but a general problem of academic research. Don Norman issued a harsh criticism on this by saying:

> I am increasingly bothered by the lack of reality in academic research...Surprisingly it often has little or no impact either upon scientific knowledge or upon society at large.... the results bear little relevance to the phenomena under study. Whether the work has any relevance to broader issues is seldom addressed. This is a common problem in the human and social sciences, where the phenomena are especially complex, variable, and heavily influenced by context.

Others support this argumentation and criticise the artificiality of research and demand for *research in the wild* [2], because of the little impacts on everyday life brought about by the detection of small differences in carefully controlled experimental settings. Another argument adding to the big picture was issued by [3] who emphasizes the tendency to quantitative, experimental evaluations with decreasing average numbers of participants and an increase of students as test subjects, the latter

© Springer International Publishing Switzerland 2015
G. Leitner, *The Future Home is Wise, Not Smart*, Computer Supported
Cooperative Work, DOI 10.1007/978-3-319-23093-1_6

meanwhile being the majority in quantitative experimental evaluations. All these aspects contribute to increasing the distance between research results gained from laboratories and their relevance in regards to computers integrated in the lives of everyone [4]. Lab-based usability evaluation under controlled conditions is applied as the gold standard of HCI methods, but, as [5] point out, *when done by rule rather than by thought*, it might be even *considered harmful*.

Despite the persistent criticism, a surprisingly high percentage of smart home research is carried out in environments and under circumstances that cannot be considered comparable to real world living conditions. For example, as [4, 6–8] point out, studies on smart homes are conducted in showrooms or laboratories that are not regularly occupied. Such environments are suitable for the exploration of basic usability issues [9, 10] and the application of *"one night stand"* methods, as [10] abel isolated usability evaluations. They are typically missing contextual similarities to the environments they are designed to emulate. The complexity and multidimensionality of the home is difficult, if not impossible, to simulate in laboratory environments [9]. It is therefore questionable to apply results achieved in laboratories to the usage of computing technology integrated into everyone's lives [4] and related experimental aspects [11]. A review of [12] addressing the cost/benefit ratio of lab vs. field based evaluations concludes, that it *"is worth the hassle"* to go into the field and to do situated research on a longitudinal basis. In the same sense [1] demands an exploitation phase which should follow the currently-prevalent exploration phase. Increasing movements in this direction are observable in the main stream of HCI, demanding a departure from the conventional orientation and from the methods and concepts which do not adequately cover the dimensions of current and future forms of human-computer interaction.

In regards to the home context, there is a need for both a reorientation on aspects influencing the adoption of technology that go beyond the technical ones, and alternative methods of research [13–15].

This collection of aspects constitute the basic drivers for the empirical founding of the WISE approach. Our work was divided into preparatory theoretical and conceptual work described in the previous chapters of this book and in [16, 17]. This became the basis for the empirical work described in [18–22] and built the basis of this chapter.

As in Chap. 2 where HCI serves as the leading theoretical concept, this chapter starts with Usability Engineering (UE), which represents the applied part of HCI.

Usability as a theoretical concept is defined in the (ISO 9241-11, 1998 [23]) norm as:

> The extent to which a product can be used by specified users to achieve specified goals with effectiveness, efficiency, and satisfaction in a specified context of use.

Because of the abstractedness of this definition a step of operationalisation is required to derive a methodological basis for the empirical approach to the WISE home. Towards this end, we apply the model of van Welie [24]. The model unravels the abstract dimensions of usability into bite-sized components and opposes them to other concepts and models existing in the HCI/Usability Engineering (UE) field,

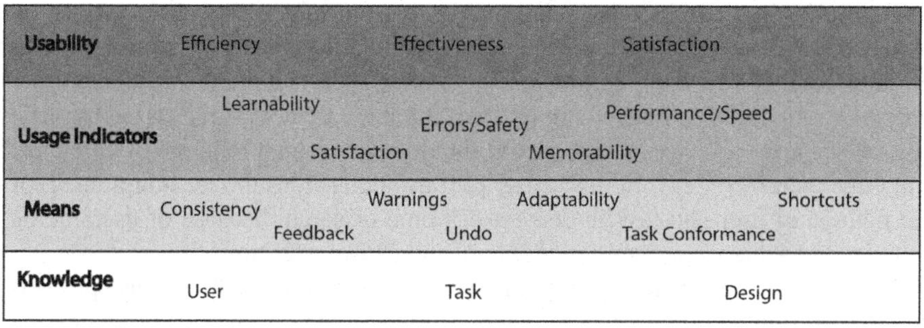

Usability	Efficiency		Effectiveness		Satisfaction	
Usage Indicators	Learnability		Errors/Safety		Performance/Speed	
		Satisfaction		Memorability		
Means	Consistency		Warnings	Adaptability		Shortcuts
		Feedback	Undo		Task Conformance	
Knowledge	User		Task		Design	

Fig. 6.1   A layered model of usability (Adapted from [24])

such as those of Shneiderman, Nielsen or Dix et al. The achievement of [24] is a layered model that breaks down the relevant related work to a more concrete level and helps "... *to achieve good usability in practice", [24, p. 619].* The basic layer of the model emphasises appropriate know-how as a prerequisite for the enhancement of the usability of a system. This is know-how about the user, about design principles of the platform the system is developed for, and an understanding of the tasks a user has to accomplish with the system. The *means* to achieve good usability (for example feedback or consistency) and *indicators* for good usability (for example, learnability) are represented in the upper layers of the model. An adequate consideration of all the elements included in the lower layers should finally result in an enhanced level of usability and its dimensions (efficiency, effectiveness and satisfaction) of the topmost layer (Fig. 6.1).

The ISO definition and the more detailed model of [24] are static models illustrating the dimensions that potentially contribute to usability. To achieve or to enhance the usability of a system, a structured process including appropriate methods has to be followed. This could either be a process oriented on a conventional software engineering approach or on an agile process. An example of the former is the usability engineering life cycle presented by [25]. The cycle starts with a requirements phase (similar to the first layer of the van Welie model), within which user characteristics, characteristics of the platform, and characteristics of tasks are elicited. Based on the results, usability goals are formulated with the intent that they are to be achieved and evaluated during the process.

The next phase is the design/test/development phase within which the system is developed iteratively, through three levels of design activities. It starts with the development and evaluation of conceptual model designs, is followed by the development of design standards and finishes with detailed user interface design. If the system has satisfactorily passed the evaluation procedures which are an integral part of the iterations, then it is deployed.

In the past, UE proved to be a good guideline for improvements to interactions with computerized systems. Several limitations with this approach drew criticism. One such criticism is an overly-strong focus on instrumental aspects [26] of interaction, which are especially correlated to the dimensions efficiency and effectiveness.

These dimensions can be considered highly relevant in contexts characterized by clearly defined and delineated procedures, typically prevalent in work contexts. But in other contexts, such as the home, *experiential* aspects can be considered more important. As has been pointed out in Chap. 3 homes are not characterized by strict tasks flows and sequences which would should be measured in terms of efficiency and effectiveness [9, 27]. In this sense, [28] even questions the meaningfulness of the notions of user and task in context of home research, because of users being singular and static while families are plural and evolve over time.

Initiatives gained momentum aiming to replace usability with a concept overcoming its limitations: user experience (UX). User experience incorporates the basic dimensions of usability but puts a specific focus on aspects that influence and contribute to the experience of technology use. This includes, for example, hedonic and affective aspects [26, p. 91]. Because of its broader approach, UX is taken as one essential foundation of the methodological approach of the WISE concept. The ISO-definition of UX (ISO 9241-210) [29] is *"... a persons perceptions and responses that result from the use or anticipated use of a product, system or service"*. The ISO norm also includes a process model, (the former ISO-13407 user centred design process) which specifies the processes to be followed to achieve UX, an iterative model with similarities to the usability engineering lifecycle of [25]. However, as with Usability Engineering, UX requires an operationalizational step if it is to be applied in an empirical process. A more detailed description of UX by [26, p. 95] serves as a starting point. The definition says that:

> User Experience is a consequence of a user's internal state (predispositions, expectations, needs, motivation, mood, etc.), the characteristics of the designed system (e.g. complexity, purpose, usability, functionality, etc.) and the context (or the environment) within which the interaction occurs (e.g. organisational/social setting, meaningfulness of the activity, voluntariness of use, etc.).

This description of UX contains many important aspects and dimensions which were considered relevant in the theoretical discussion of WISE. These are aspects of the technology, the human and the environment, also covered in the wisdom concept of [30]. Another important parallel to wisdom is that UX covers long-term aspects by explicitly addressing not only the usage situation itself, but also the relevant phases before (anticipation) and after (reflection) a concrete usage. Facets of UX are shown in Table 6.1.

Table 6.1 An overview on facets of user experience (Adapted from [26])

Beyond the instrumental	holistic, aesthetic, hedonic
Emotion and affect	subjective, positive, antecedents and consequences
The Experiental	dynamic, complex, unique, situated, temporally-bounded

What UX lacks, in comparison to the wisdom model, is the explicit reference to values, although they are implicitly covered. But putting the emphasis on values is important because value systems are essential elements of life at home [31, 32]. Their relevance has also led to recent changes in the orientation of HCI [15, 33]. One observable consequence of this change is the introduction of a new phase in the iterative process which builds a central element of HCI-related process models, for example [25] and [29] presented earlier. This new phase is *understanding*, and it aims at addressing phenomena such as values. To understand the context and the value system characterizing the circumstances under which an interactive system is used is an indispensable prerequisite of the whole process.

6.1 The WISE Process Model

As a consequence of the criticism of the methodological limits of past smart home research, the central goal of WISE is the deployment of technology into both field research and real world living environments. This represents a clear contrast to research performed exclusively in artificial environments, but this contrast is also characterized by specific challenges. The first is that it would be inappropriate to deploy technology directly into real-world settings without ensuring that the technology is truly suitable for that setting. Otherwise the users are degraded into beta-testers. Another requirement is that the deployment (and evaluation) of the technology follows a slow, *piecemeal* [34] approach in order to avoid disturbing the sensitive ecosystems of real living environments and overexerting their inhabitants. We propose a process model in order to address these issues. Our model is an extension and combination of the process models previously expounded by [25, 29] with some consideration of the stages of maturity of the technology that will be developed – either initially or as a continuum. The process has three stages (research facilities; living labs/model homes; real world contexts) within which iterations similar to those included in the usability engineering lifecycle or UX [25, 29] are performed. The model treats [15]'s presentation of *understand* as essential to situated research. This activity is addressed in the WISE process by a thorough analysis of contextual conditions and values, and through the involvement of relevant stakeholders in the respective phases. After a system (or a subsystem, prototype, or single device) has undergone iterations and achieved a certain level of maturity, the next stage is entered. In each stage of the process model shown in Fig. 6.2 the same principle elements are applied: understanding; requirement elicitation; design; and evaluation. The difference is in the concrete methods that are applied.

A more detailed description of the stages is given in the following subsections, with references to related work and our own empirical work performed in relation to the stages. The focus is put on the last stage – field deployment – because it is considered the central stage of the WISE approach. As a result, the research contributions that we could achieve in relation to this stage are considered the most important.

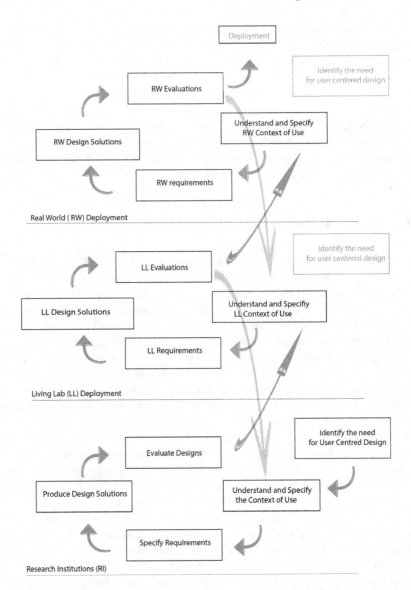

Fig. 6.2 WISE Process Model – the model is based on iterations starting at the bottom (*Identify the need for user centred design*). With the application of appropriate methods, a higher level of maturity of the developed (prototype) system is achieved. The first stage is research institutions (RI), the second stage is living labs and model homes (LL), the final stage is real world (RW) deployment

6.1.1 Stage 1: Research Institutions

First-stage facilities include offices and labs in research institutions where soft-
or hardware prototypes are developed and initially evaluated regarding their user
experience. The product to be designed could, for example, be a smart home wall-
mounted control panel, intended for use in a home setting. After starting the human
centred design process, the specification of the context of use is done, but may leave
out aspects which are not relevant in this stage, or not known. It is not important
to define where exactly the panel should be mounted. A general phrase such as *in
a central location in the home* may be satisfactory in this stage. In later stages,
this would of course have to be replaced with a more specific definition. The same
difference applies with the specification of other requirements. The focus of this
stage are – in relation to the founding concepts wisdom and UX – the characteristics
of the system (usability and functional range). User characteristics (e.g. motivation,
expectations) and contextual conditions do not, in general, play such an important
role. Therefore the methodologies of choice are, for example, standard usability
tests. Due to the orientation of the stage subjects participating in evaluations may
differ to a certain extent from the final target group, in terms of their characteristics.
They could be recruited from a student population, as this is usually done in such a
context [3]. The stage is characterized by hypothesis-driven experimental methods,
performed under controlled conditions, and aimed at the systematic collection of
predominantly quantitative data. Instrumental aspects, classical usability criteria
such as effectiveness and efficiency are in the focus; measured by metrics such as
degree of task completion, time for task performance and number of errors. The
subjective opinions of the test subjects are collected with standard questionnaires.
The data are further processed and analysed using quantitative statistical methods.
When a system is developed from scratch, then, of course, this requires more than
one iteration ([25], for example, proposes three) and an adequate combination of
design and evaluation methods. Conceptual model designs based on paper mock-
ups as design solutions would be an appropriate method for the first iteration, the
digitization of which would follow in the next iterations. An overview of standard
methodology to be applied in this stage can be found in [35–37]. Examples of our
empirical work related to this stage are described in [17, 20, 38]. The outcomes of
the stage are functional prototypes, that have been iteratively fine-tuned, and that are
on their way to being ready to be deployed to the next stage, living labs and model
homes.

At this point it is important to start an attempt to bridge the gap between the
expressed criticism of some areas of research and the WISE approach. The problems
emphasised in the introduction of this chapter should not be misunderstood as a
statement that other research was, in general, following the wrong path. In the
context of the first stage of the WISE approach this kind of research has its rationale,
when considering it as representing a first stage of a bigger process. As will be
emphasised in Sect. 6.1.4, this has the benefit that the further stages of research can
build upon existing results instead of having to start from scratch or to re-invent the
wheel.

6.1.2 Stage 2: Living Labs/Model Homes

After the successful completion of the first stage, the mature system prototype enters the next stage; the stage of living labs and model homes. These environments are characterized by an infrastructure that is comparable to the research institutions of the first stage but that also have some commonalities with real living environments. This combination allows the execution of simulations by providing conditions under which users can perform more complex, and thus more realistic, interactions with the technology and with the environment. Evaluations that are conducted in this stage are designed with a broader focus. Instrumental aspects are no longer the sole point of interest. The focus of UX expands to embrace the interplay between users and devices. As was emphasized in the discussion of the first stage, there is also a large body of past work representing this stage; a body upon which one can build in order to reach the next stage more quickly.

Many of the lighthouse projects in smart home research (e.g. The Aware Home, house_n, iHomeLab, InHaus, to mention only a few) draw on such facilities. They have taken big leaps forward and yielded many valuable outcomes in smart home research [39, 40]. An advantage of these environments is that the people participating in the experiment can stay there for a longer period of time. The methods applied shift from fully controlled experimental settings into variants and combinations of observational and interview methods. Participants still may be students, but if more interpersonal and group phenomena are to be observed the participants have to be similar to the target group. Examples of methods that can be applied at this stage are provided in [37, 41].

Although facilities representing this second stage support a broader variety of research, they are still somewhat artificial, because people typically stay there just for research purposes rather than for the purpose of long term dwelling. This precludes the option of gathering the depth of information that would have to be considered in the complex context of a real home environment. Our own work corresponding to this stage was carried out in a living lab facility and studies performed in this environment focused on the further development of the WISE software platform. For example, one series of studies analysed the possibilities of integrating speech and gesture as alternative modes of interaction with a home, representing a variant of calm interaction. A more detailed description of the test design and the results can be found in [18] and [22]. Other work representing this stage was the development and evaluation of an interface prototype for iOS-based tablets and smart phones [42] or the possibilities of visualizing energy consumption [43].

Another facility played a specific role in our work and can be considered as a hybrid location somewhere inbetween living labs and field environments. The location designated household 37 (HH37)[1] is my own home and served as a

---

[1]In the course of establishing the WISE software platform, research facilities such as labs and real world households were sequentially connected. In some cases, when a significant extension was made, the research entity received a new ID. HH37 is the ID of the most current expansion level of my own home.

parallel R&D location significantly different from research facilities, as well as an intermediate stage for the deployment of the WISE platform in the field. HH37 still serves as a basis for specific research activities for which other locations are not appropriate. Examples of first attempts of research based on HH37 are described in [19] and [44]. The need to conduct research in one's own living environment is a consequence of the low dissemination of smart technology mentioned in the previous chapters. Facilities which are appropriately equipped and provide the possibility of thorough investigations under real world conditions are specifically hard to find. Because of this limitation, other pioneering work in smart home research also took place in the living environment of the researcher. One such example is the adaptive home [45]. A detailed description of the research carried out in HH37 will be provided in Chap. 7.

6.1.3 Stage 3: Field Environments

The final and at once most important stage in the WISE process is conducted in real world environments. As has been emphasized, the previous two stages simply cannot cover the whole range of aspects that are relevant. Values and other aspects that characterize *the embodiment of interaction* [46], require a *situated perspective* [15, 31] in order to be thoroughly understood. It has been pointed out by [47] that ethnographic and longitudinal studies help to highlight the nature of domestic activities, the need for future technology to be sympathetic to everyday routine. As an example, consider the use of the Internet for leisure activities and its impact on specific user groups such as children. Cultural probes and other similar data acquisition techniques highlight the need to be sensitive to a broader set of characteristics, such as the values that influence life at home; characteristics which are quite different from those traditionally associated with work-oriented settings.

At this stage, the focus of UX expands to take a broader context and long-term aspects into account. It constitutes a specific challenge to examine such aspects of interaction, how technology integrates into the life of its users, in the sense of Culkin, Churchill or Sternberg, how it *shapes* the living circumstances. In contrast to the locations where the other two stages take place, the environments in which this stage is conducted cannot be assumed to be equipped with appropriate technology. Before being able to perform research under these circumstances, the initial task is therefore to deploy a basic technical infrastructure to the environment where research is conducted. A detailed discussion of deployment issues is provided in [18]. While stressing the importance of researching technology in the home [27] points out the related difficulties because homes typically do not easily accommodate specific technical equipment. What differentiates our approach from others in the field is that we have concentrated our efforts on developing a modular platform which supports easy retrofitting and enables a piecemeal approach [34] which in turn allows for the evaluation of a variety of functionalities and applications. This is possible just by exchanging singular devices or subsystems, rather than building stand-alone prototypes or devices [15]. This strategy supports addressing a variety of research questions in combination with different evaluation methods. For an overview of fieldwork methods, see, for example [35, 48]. An important self-imposed requirement which can be considered as another facet of WISE was that the deployment itself, as well as the research methods applied, should be as reserved and unobtrusive as possible. Therefore methods applied in the living lab or in HH37 (for example observations based on cameras) would not be appropriate. Thus, as described in more detail in [18], a reasonable quantity and quality of machine-generated data can also be achieved with environmental sensors. As an additional source of information to test hypotheses and conclusions, these data are complemented by socio-psychological methods, as described in [41, 49].

The methodological focus of this stage moves away from experimental design and controlled conditions. Instead, the focus is on a thorough *understanding* of the individual contextual conditions made possible via the generation of qualitative data with a lower relevance to classical quality criteria (such as replicability, objectivity and generalizability), but with a gain in ecological validity. A hypothesis-driven and hypothesis-testing approach is exchanged for a qualitative data collection, categorization, and hypothesis-generation, such as is proposed, for example, in grounded theory [48, 50]. An example for a methodological orientation is sketched in [49] which constitutes a combination of the technology acceptance model (TAM), the method of contextual inquiry and social network analysis. The TAM, for example, offers the possibility to operationalize needs and motivations, emphasised as one of the relevant human aspects in regard to the smart home in Chap. 2 .

The humanities have a long history of field-based research which should be reconsidered in state-of-the-art smart home research. I remember when I first came into contact with this kind of research during my undergraduate studies. I was very impressed by a pioneering example of sociological field research that took place in Austria, the Marienthal study [51], and the insights that could be gained from this kind of research. Similar approaches are found in the philosophical tradition of phenomenology [52] and sociological ethnomethodology [46] which build a clear contrast to, as [46] labels it – *"armchair research"* – and helped build an understanding not just of what people do, but of what they experience in the doing [46].

In the context of HCI, the field of CSCW has provided a reasonable grounding in the use of ethnographic methodology [15, 31]. The variety of methods to be applied in this stage is big. The major challenge is to find a balance between collecting enough data and limiting the degree to which we disturb the ecosystem of private living environments. An unnecessary amount of interference in the environment could potentially corrupt the data causing a *Hawthorne effect* or some other aberration. Examples of methods that can be applied in this stage are presented in [41, 49]. However, there is a diversity, not only in regard to the theoretical methods to build upon, but also in regard to the technical means to support evaluations at this stage. The unobtrusiveness of our approach was also important in this regard. The challenge was, for example, to find a compromise between the least intrusive means for recording- paper and pen – and that which might enable the easiest re-use of collected data – such as laptops, dictaphones, or cameras.

In the context of HH37 a variety of devices and methods were tested. Examples include web and smartphone apps and cameras worn on a lanyard, which took pictures periodically in order to provide contextual information to support data analysis. The best solution for the support of field work could be found in a system named Livescribe (R). It looks like a paper and pen, but both the paper and the pen really deserve to be called *smart*. Handwritten notes generated with this system are automatically digitized and can be stored and shared easily. Moreover, the pen enables audio recording saved in mp3 format. In this way it is possible to record meetings without disturbing the flow of a conversation. This, is as opposed to a laptop building a barrier between the interviewee and interviewer, for example, but it still provides the benefits of digital technology. Results from our own work in this final stage emphasize the importance of conducting research that is at once, both *field-based* and *long-term*. One example of this is described in [18].

6.1.4   Iterative Approach

The principal sequence of the process model is the one that was described, but it is also possible for the movement between stages to be reversed. A field trial may, for example, reveal that the interaction modality of a prototype does not fit into the contextual conditions of the environment. Then the process goes back to one of the earlier stages and an alternative prototype is developed and evaluated in the research facility, before being evaluated again in the living lab and, eventually, reaching the stage of field deployment again. It is also possible (and even probable) that not all stages have to be passed through by one and the same researcher or group. Concepts and systems from other groups, having already passed earlier stages, can then be taken forward into a new stage. This would be an appropriate approach considering the ample literature in the field. This strategy was also applied in the project described in Chap. 7 and in [18]. The WISE platform is conceptualized to support such a flexibility. However, taking into consideration the benefits of the WISE platform such as modularity, openness and adaptability, the biggest advantage is achieved when the whole process is performed on the same technical basis; a platform that is either present or can be retrofitted into almost arbitrary contexts. In this way, customization and adaptation efforts can be reduced.

References

1. Solaimani, S., Bouwman, H., & Baken, N. (2011). The smart home landscape: A qualitative meta-analysis. In *Toward useful services for elderly and people with disabilities* (pp. 192–199). Berlin/Heidelberg: Springer.
2. Boring, R. L. (2002, September). Human-computer interaction as cognitive science. In *Proceedings of the Human Factors and Ergonomics Society Annual Meeting*, Maryland (Vol. 46, No. 21, pp. 1767–1771). SAGE Publications.

3. Barkhuus, L., & Rode, J. A. (2007, April). From Mice to Men-24 years of evaluation in CHI. In *Proceedings of the SIGCHI Conference on Human Factors in Computing Systems*, San Jose. ACM.

4. Brush, A. J., Lee, B., Mahajan, R., Agarwal, S., Saroiu, S., & Dixon, C. (2011, May). Home automation in the wild: Challenges and opportunities. In *Proceedings of the SIGCHI Conference on Human Factors in Computing Systems*, Vancouver (pp. 2115–2124). ACM.

5. Greenberg, S., & Buxton, B. (2008, April). Usability evaluation considered harmful (some of the time). In *Proceedings of the SIGCHI Conference on Human Factors in Computing Systems*, Florence (pp. 111–120). ACM.

6. Ding, D., Cooper, R. A., Pasquina, P. F., & Fici-Pasquina, L. (2011). Sensor technology for smart homes. *Maturitas, 69*(2), 131–136.

7. Mennicken, S., & Huang, E. M. (2012). Hacking the natural habitat: An in-the-wild study of smart homes, their development, and the people who live in them. In *Pervasive computing* (pp. 143–160). Berlin/Heidelberg: Springer.

8. Kensing, F., & Blomberg, J. (1998). Participatory design: Issues and concerns. *Computer Supported Cooperative Work (CSCW), 7*(3–4), 167–185.

9. Takayama, L., Pantofaru, C., Robson, D., Soto, B., & Barry, M. (2012). Making technology homey: Finding sources of satisfaction and meaning in home automation. In *Proceedings of the 2012 ACM Conference on Ubiquitous Computing*, Pittsburgh (pp. 511–520). ACM.

10. Rode, J. A., Toye, E. F., & Blackwell, A. F. (2004). The fuzzy felt ethnography – Understanding the programming patterns of domestic appliances. *Personal and Ubiquitous Computing, 8*(3–4), 161–176.

11. Norman, D. A. (1993). *Things that make us smart: Defending human attributes in the age of the machine*. Reading, MA: Addison Wesley Publishers.

12. Kjeldskov, J., & Skov, M. B. (2014). Was it worth the Hassle? Ten years of mobile HCI research discussions on lab and field evaluations. In *16th International Conference on Human-Computer Interaction with Mobile Devices and Services (Mobile HCI)*, Toronto.

13. Mennicken, S., Vermeulen, J., & Huang, E. M. (2014). From today's augmented houses to tomorrow's smart homes: New directions for home automation research. In *Proceedings of the 2014 ACM International Joint Conference on Pervasive and Ubiquitous Computing* (pp. 105–115). New York: ACM.

14. Kjeldskov, J., Skov, M. B., Als, B. S., & Høegh, R. T. (2004). Is it worth the hassle? Exploring the added value of evaluating the usability of context-aware mobile systems in the field. In *Mobile human-computer interaction-MobileHCI 2004* (pp. 61–73). Berlin/Heidelberg: Springer.

15. Harper, R. H. (2008). *Being human: Human-computer interaction in the year 2020*. Cambridge: Microsoft Research Limited.

16. Leitner, G., Hitz, M., Fercher, A. J., & Brown, J. N. (2013). Aspekte der human computer interaction im smart home. *HMD Praxis der Wirtschaftsinformatik, 50*(6), 37–47.

17. Felfernig, A., Friedrich, G., Gula, B., Hitz, M., Kruggel, T., Leitner, G., Melcher, R., Riepan, D., Strauss, S. Teppan, E. & Vitouch, O. (2007). Persuasive recommendation: Serial position effects in knowledge-based recommender systems. In *Persuasive technology* (pp. 283–294). Berlin/Heidelberg: Springer.

18. Leitner, G., Felfernig, A., Fercher, A. J., & Hitz, M. (2014). Disseminating ambient assisted living in rural areas. *Sensors, Special Issue Ambient Assisted Living, 14*(8), 13496–13531.

19. Leitner, G., Hitz, M., & Ahlström, D. (2007). Applicability and usability of off-the-shelf smart appliances in tele-care. In *21st International Conference on Advanced Information Networking and Applications Workshops, 2007 (AINAW'07)*, Niagara Falls (Vol. 2, pp. 881–886). IEEE.

20. Leitner, G., Ahlström, D., & Hitz, M. (2007). Usability of mobile computing in emergency response systems – Lessons learned and future directions. In *HCI and usability for medicine and health care* (LNCS 4799, pp. 241–254). Springer: Berlin/Heidelberg.

21. Ayuningtyas, C. *Activity modeling for multi-user environments*. Ph.D. Thesis. Erasmus Mundus Doctorate Program in Interactive and Cognitive Environments (ICE), Alpen Adria Universität Klagenfurt. Work in progress.

22. Brown, J. N. A. (2014). *Unifying interaction across distributed controls in a smart environment using anthropology-based computing to make human-computer interaction "Calm"*. Ph.D. Thesis, Erasmus Mundus Doctorate Program in Interactive and Cognitive Environments (ICE), Alpen Adria Universität Klagenfurt, Austria.

23. ISO, W. (1998). *9241-11. Ergonomic requirements for office work with visual display terminals (VDTs)*. Geneva: The International Organization for Standardization.

24. Van Welie, M., Van Der Veer, G. C., & Eliëns, A. (1999, September). Breaking down usability. In *Proceedings of INTERACT*, Amsterdam (Vol. 99, pp. 613–620).

25. Mayhew, D. J. (1999). *The usability engineering lifecycle: A practitioner's guide to user interface design*. San Francisco: Morgan Kaufmann.

26. Hassenzahl, M., & Tractinsky, N. (2006). User experience-a research agenda. *Behaviour and Information Technology, 25*(2), 91–97.

27. Hindus, D. (1999). The importance of homes in technology research. In *Cooperative buildings. Integrating information, organizations, and architecture* (pp. 199–207). Berlin/Heidelberg: Springer.

28. Davidoff, S., Lee, M. K., Yiu, C., Zimmerman, J., & Dey, A. K. (2006). Principles of smart home control. In *UbiComp: Ubiquitous computing* (pp. 19–34). Berlin/Heidelberg: Springer.

29. DIS, I. (2009). *9241-210: 2010. Ergonomics of human system interaction-Part 210: Human-centred design for interactive systems*. Geneva: International Standardization Organization (ISO).

30. Sternberg, R. J. (2004). What is wisdom and how can we develop it? *The Annals of the American Academy of Political and Social Science, 591*(1), 164–174.

31. Harrison, S., Tatar, D., & Sengers, P. (2007). The three paradigms of HCI. In *Alt. Chi. Session at the SIGCHI Conference on Human Factors in Computing Systems*, San Jose (pp. 1–18).

32. Cockton, G. (2004). Value-centred HCI. In *Proceedings of the Third Nordic Conference on Human-Computer Interaction*, Tampere (pp. 149–160). ACM.

33. Bannon, L. (2011). Reimagining HCI: Toward a more human-centered perspective. *Interactions, 18*(4), 50–57.

34. Edwards, W. K., & Grinter, R. E. (2001). At home with ubiquitous computing: Seven challenges. In *Ubicomp: Ubiquitous computing* (pp. 256–272). Berlin/Heidelberg: Springer.

35. Lazar, J., Feng, J. H., & Hochheiser, H. (2010). *Research methods in human-computer interaction*. New Jersey: Wiley.

36. Nielsen, J. (1994). *Usability engineering*. Amsterdam: Elsevier.

37. Sauro, J., & Lewis, J. R. (2012). *Quantifying the user experience: Practical statistics for user research*. Amsterdam: Elsevier.

38. Leitner, G., Fercher, A. J., & Lassen, C. (2013). End users programming smart homes – A case study on scenario programming. In *Human-computer interaction and knowledge discovery in complex, unstructured, big data* (pp. 217–236). Berlin/Heidelberg: Springer.

39. Chan, M., Estéve, D., Escriba, C., & Campo, E. (2008). A review of smart homes – Present state and future challenges. *Computer Methods and Programs in Biomedicine, 91*(1), 55–81.

40. Yamazaki, T. (2006). Beyond the smart home. In *International Conference on Hybrid Information Technology, 2006 (ICHIT'06)*, Cheju Island (Vol. 2, pp. 350–355). IEEE.

41. Kray, C., Larsen, L. B., Olivier, P., Biemans, M., van Bunningen, A., Fetter, M., Jay, T., Khan, V.-J., Leitner, G., Mulder, I., Müller, J., Plötz, T., & de Vallejo, I. L. (2008). Evaluating ubiquitous systems with users (workshop summary). In *Constructing ambient intelligence* (pp. 63–74). Berlin/Heidelberg: Springer.

42. Schmidt, B. *Smart phone based interaction in smart home and AAL environments*. Diploma Thesis, Alpen-Adria Universität Klagenfurt. Work in progress.

43. Fercher, A., Hitz, M., & Leitner, G. (2009). Pervasive approaches to awareness of energy consumption. In *Ami-Blocks*, Salzburg (pp. 3–8). Erlangen, Germany.

44. Leitner, G., Ahlström, D., & Hitz, M. (2007). Usability – Key factor of future smart home systems. In *Home informatics and telematics: ICT for the next billion* (pp. 269–278). New York: Springer.

45. Mozer, M. C. (1998). The neural network house: An environment hat adapts to its inhabitants. In *Proceedings AAAI Spring Symposium on Intelligent Environments*, Menlo Park (pp. 110–114).
46. Dourish, P. (2004). *Where the action is: The foundations of embodied interaction*. Cambridge: MIT.
47. Crabtree, A., Hemmings, T., Rodden, T., Cheverst, K., Clarke, K., Dewsbury, G., & Rouncefield, M. (2003, November). Designing with care: Adapting cultural probes to inform design in sensitive settings. In *Proceedings of the 2004 Australasian Conference on Computer-Human Interaction (OZCHI2004)*, Wollongong (pp. 4–13).
48. Randall, D., Harper, R., & Rouncefield, M. (2007). *Fieldwork for design: Theory and practice*. London: Springer.
49. Leitner, G., Mitrea, O., & Fercher, A. J. (2013). Towards an acceptance model for AAL. In *Human factors in computing and informatics* (pp. 672–679). Berlin/Heidelberg: Springer.
50. Glaser, B. G., & Strauss, A. L. (2009). *The discovery of grounded theory: Strategies for qualitative research*. Transaction Publishers. New Brunswick, USA and London, UK: AldineTransaction (a Division of Transaction Publishers).
51. Jahoda, M., Lazarsfeld, P. F., & Zeisel, H. (1960). *Die Arbeitslosen von Marienthal: Ein soziographischer Versuch Äüber die Wirkungen langandauernder Arbeitslosigkeit, mit einem Anhang zur Geschichte der Soziographie* (Vol. 2). Allensbach: Verlag für Demoskopie.
52. Heidegger, M. (1952). Bauen Wohnen Denken. Vorträge und Aufsätze, 151.

Part III
The WISE Home of the Future

Chapter 7
The Proof of the WISE Concept

After the description of the theoretical foundations of the WISE paradigm and the process accompanying the WISE approach in the previous chapters, this chapter presents empirical examples, which shall be considered as a proof of concept. There are three examples given, in accordance with the WISE process model presented in Chap. 6. First we present experiments and studies carried out in lab facilities. The next example, representing the model home stage, is household 37, a real-world living environment which served as a test-bed for most of the last ten years. The final project presented, Casa Vecchia, was a longitudinal field study and represents the stage of field deployment. In the course of this ambient assisted living (AAL) project, the WISE platform was installed in more than 20 households inhabited by elderly people. The socio-psychological and technological aspects of the project were evaluated intensively over a period of four years.

7.1 University Facilities and Research Labs

As has been pointed out in the previous chapters, the goal of the WISE approach is to deploy and evaluate technology *in the wild* [1, 2]. But depending on the stage of development and maturity of the prototype system it is necessary to perform evaluations under experimental and controlled conditions before being able to deploy a system in the field. To that end, a lab facility was established on the university campus where enhancements of the WISE functionality could be developed, tested and refined. The work on smart homes in general and the WISE idea in particular first started with a theoretical contention with the topic and the formulation of research questions. In the next step it was necessary to empirically evaluate the concepts and prototypes that had been derived from the theoretical considerations. A first expansion stage of the lab facility and an initial version of the WISE platform supported this need. The system available at that time can be

© Springer International Publishing Switzerland 2015
G. Leitner, *The Future Home is Wise, Not Smart,* Computer Supported
Cooperative Work, DOI 10.1007/978-3-319-23093-1_7

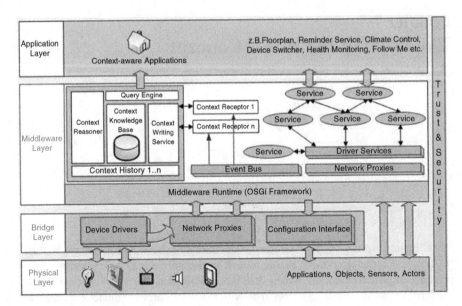

Fig. 7.1 The original WISE software architecture, developed by [3] to support the research group's activities

considered as only being *pre-wise* because it had several limitations. The principal architecture sketched in Chap. 5 was already observable but it was characterized by specifics and limitations on the hard- and software level.

The software platform is sketched in Fig. 7.1 showing the platform and the components the platform consists of. The principle elements of the platform have already been described in Chap. 5, the figure is depicting some more technical details which have to be considered to understand the detailed functionality discussed in the following examples. A detailed description of the platform can be found in [3].

The hardware platform chosen for the first prototype was a system from a German manufacturer, sold online over channels that primarily target do-it-yourselfers. It fulfilled the basic requirements enumerated in Chap. 5 such as being small in size for retrofit, communicating wirelessly, providing an acceptable variety of functions and being available for a reasonable price. Another aspect which was indicative for this system was an active community of professionals and hobbyists who supported the system and were also developing an alternative and open software, FHEM.[1] In contrast to the software that is sold with the hardware that is closed source, FHEM could be customized, and that made it possible to integrate the hardware into the WISE platform. The hardware consists of components such as sensors and actuators, remote controls and push buttons, which communicate over a proprietary

---

[1] http://fhem.de

Fig. 7.2 The customized central unit running independently on the basis of the Gateway component, a Network Bridge in combination with a harddisk exchanging the PC and a Motion Sensor as example component [3]

radio protocol with a central unit. The central unit is a gateway module, which translates the signals of the proprietary protocol into usb signals, or, in another version, into wireless LAN signals. The gateway did not work independently, but had to be attached to a personal computer running the control software. Although the software did not require much computational power, it was necessary to run the PC around the clock, seven days per week in order to keep the system operational. This shortcoming has been overcome with the development of a proprietary architecture based on a network-attached storage running Linux that was able to replace the PC. The final solution developed by [3], is shown in Fig. 7.2.

The second shortcoming of the initial hardware platform was that the components did not communicate bi-directionally. This led to the problem that the status information of the components could not be trusted. Because of the problems and constraints of the initial platform, it was exchanged by a system with a better technical basis. This hardware is distributed by the same company as the initial hardware platform and sold over the same channels. The new hardware platform already had an integrated gateway component which was able to control and run the hardware and software independently, without the need for an additional PC. The communication was bidirectional, so the status information of the attached components could be considered correct. The system also had other enhancements in regards to connectivity, such as an open software interface specification based on XML-RPC, a better fault tolerance, and better stability. The transfer between the two different hardware platforms was the first practical test for the WISE architecture and it demonstrated that the platform can cope with different hardware platforms and software components. Because the new system had only recently been introduced to the market it did not cover the same range of functionality as the initial one. It was therefore necessary to run the two systems in parallel. Despite the weaknesses of the initial system it was considered better to have some functionality (even with technical limitations) instead of going without it. Being able to run two systems in parallel was another demonstration of the flexibility and adaptability of the platform. Another hardware system that was integrated into the WISE platform was a powerline operated smart home platform from Switzerland developed in cooperation with the ETH Zurich. The system had the benefit of running on the standard electric wiring of a building which would result in several advantages. Compared to wireless systems, no interference with other wireless devices or range problems caused by building structures would have to be expected. Because the signals are modulated on the existing wiring, no additional wires have to be installed, as would have been the case with bus-operated wired smart home systems. These advantages motivated us to use the powerline system in the context of the ambient assisted living project described later in this chapter. However, because of delays in the certification for the Austrian market we were not able to deploy components of the powerline platform in the field. Finally, the WISE platform was adapted to integrate the Arduino® smartboard platform, which enabled the development of customized components providing functionality not available in the other hardware platforms at our disposal. With the release of the WISE platform it was possible to carry out first feasibility studies in the lab facilities. According to the WISE process model presented in Chap. 6, the studies were merely focussed on basic interaction and usability aspects. The central question addressed within the lab facility was: *How could smart home systems be made more usable and useful; supporting instrumental needs such as effectiveness and efficiency,* primarily in cooperation with students, a large amount of research work was carried out to address these problems. For example, a project focusing on indoor location with low-cost components was done by [4], potentials of multi-user support was investigated by [5], and [6] focussed her work on activity pattern recognition, to mention only a few.

The two studies presented in more detail were not performed as initial steps in a development process. They are examples of the possibility to change the sequence, as proposed in the description of the WISE process model in Chap. 6. The need to perform the studies developed from experiences gained in the field projects presented later in this chapter. Based on those experiences and the elicited requirements, prototypes were developed which were to be tested before being deployed to the field again.

The first study presented addressed the question of whether it would make sense to enable the inhabitants of smart homes to perform not only basic control tasks, but even more complex tasks, such as programming their homes themselves [7]. The goal was to evaluate the possibilities in regard to the predictions of [8] who proposed that the orientation of HCI would move from the era of *easy to use* to the era of *easy to develop*, resulting in a higher need for end user development. The feature we evaluated was scenario programming. A scenario can be described as a person's activity which is performed frequently and involves a number of things and devices. These can also be electric, electronic and computerized devices, for example, when a person wants to watch TV. In a conventional home, it would be necessary for the person to separately close blinds or curtains, dim the lights, switch on the TV, and select the correct channel. In a smart home this could be done in a combined way, optimally with the press of only one button. But such a combined control of devices has to be pre-programmed in state-of-the-art smart home systems. We were interested whether naïve users would be interested and able to do this kind of pre-programming.

The study had two stages. In a pre-study, we investigated whether scenarios in general are in the interest of users or if they are just another example of a technological solution in search of a problem. To be able to answer this question 18 participants were interviewed regarding their daily activities in the home, in order to see if there was any routine behaviour that could reasonably be supported by smart home functionality and combined in scenarios. In order to focus the attention of the participants on their behaviour rather than on technical capabilities, we did not, at first, inform them about the real purpose of the investigation. They were just informed that we would be interested in the frequency and regularity of activities that take place at home. In the first phase of the investigation the participants were asked about the activities that take place in general, and if there are any activities or sequences of activities that are carried out on a regular basis. This interview revealed that 100 % of the participants have a morning routine which is the same every day, specifically on weekdays. Around 40 % stated that there are other routine activities which are also characterized by recurring sequences. They are performed when they leave home, come home or do cleaning, receiving guests, preparing a journey, cooking, or preparing to go out.

As routines seem to be quite common, the second phase of the study was devoted to the question of how these routines could be supported by smart home functionality. It was carried out as a card sorting experiment, but not in the usual way, to just stack cards that are considered as having something in common. The cards had to be put in a sequence which corresponded to the routine the devices are involved in. Each of the roughly 30 cards showed an object that is typically present in a home, the majority of which were electric appliances, such as home appliances, entertainment and computing devices. Furniture and infrastructural components (e.g. radiators) were also depicted. Figure 7.3 shows an example of the material provided.

The result of the pre-study revealed that routines are an important part in the daily activities, and are closely related to devices. If the devices were integrated into a smart home system, their integration into scenarios would make sense. This motivated the performance of a follow-up study in the lab. The study was based on a prototype that was developed in Android to run on a tablet computer. Because the participants of the pre-study reported that they had found the interaction with the cards and the time sequence templates quite intuitive, the goal for the prototype was to simulate this interaction on the tablet in a digitized form. The fact that tablets are operated by touch interaction supported this goal. The prototype was evaluated in a comparative study with the interfaces of two commercial smart

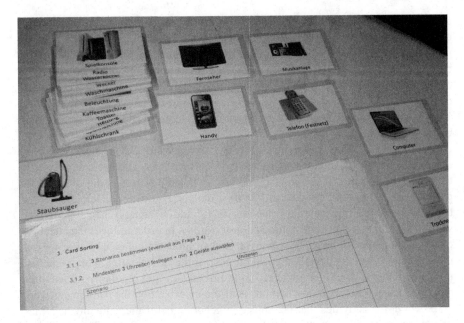

Fig. 7.3 Material provided for the performance of the pretest

home software products. In this study 17 participants were asked to program two scenarios, alternating with the three interfaces. The following questions were addressed. First, we wanted to find the specific characteristics of, and the differences between, the three systems (usability, utility, appeal, etc.) Second, we wanted to find out how well our prototype would perform in comparison to commercial systems. It was of specific interest to see how well people would perform with the three systems without training. The following paragraph describes one of the scenarios the participants had to program.

Scenarios 1: Morning activity.
Please imagine that you want to program your smart home so that it performs the following functions: After you get up (and open the door of your bedroom) the heating in the bathroom is raised to 25° Celsius and 10 minutes later the coffee maker is activated in the kitchen. A screenshot of the study prototype is shown in Fig. 7.4.

Objective metrics such as time for completion of the tasks, number and characteristics of errors and degree of completion were recorded, combined with subjective measures that were collected with the UEQ questionnaire [9]. In summary the objective measures revealed that our prototype was in about the same range as the commercial systems. Complete failures in task completion did not only occur with our prototype but also with the commercial systems. On the subjective level the results also revealed that our prototype system is generally felt to be equal to the others. We had expected that our system, being a prototype and unfamiliar to

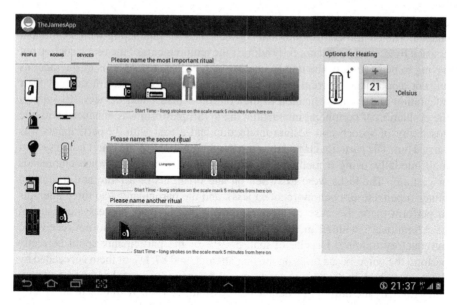

Fig. 7.4 The prototype for the main study. On the left hand side a tabbed container is provided which contains the source elements needed to program a scenario. Most important elements are the devices, but we also provided elements representing two other categories, rooms and people, because these could also be relevant for the configuration of a scenario. With Drag&Drop the elements can be positioned in one of the three containers in the centre which include a time grid to configure three different scenarios as sequences

the participant, would perform significantly worse than the commercial systems, and that it would be perceived as being significantly worse. The fact that it was generally equal in performance and in qualitative evaluation confirms the assumption expressed throughout this book that user needs are not being appropriately recognized and met in smart home products available on the market. Otherwise the commercial systems would have been able to outperform our prototypical solution. We also take this as evidence that the WISE approach and process model are at least pointing in the right direction.

Another series of studies was performed in the lab environment in an attempt to analyse the use of alternative modalities such as speech or gesture to interact with an appropriately equipped home environment. The motivation for these studies is related to the drawbacks of state-of-the-art smart home systems which do not appropriately consider human capabilities. One example of the capabilities being ignored is presented in our discussion of attentional processes, which is emphasised in Chap. 2. Two research activities contributed to the design of the study, both of them related to attentional processes, or more concretely, to the concept of calm computing. One is the work of my colleague JNA Brown [10] who was analysing how interaction with a smart home could be broken down into a generic and intuitive set of commands that can be issued multi-modally and peripherally, for example, by using gestures and voice commands. The other motivation for the studies was derived from the Casa Vecchia project, which is described in detail later in this chapter. The central control unit that was designed for interacting with an ambient assisted living system did not fully address the requirements of the users, such as not having to be in front of the unit to interact with it. Peripheral forms of interactions are not available in current smart homes, but the WISE platform enables their integration and their application to the control of distributed devices. To support the evaluation of peripheral interaction, the WISE platform was enhanced with the possibility of speech and gesture interaction and a trial with 32 participants was carried out. The participants had to control eight functions of the smart home system multi-modally, using a method that focussed mainly on either voice commands or gestures. The tasks were to switch on and off lights or a radio and to control blinds (open, close, open more, open less), and the participants had three attempts to perform them. Because of the requirement that a smart home system should work intuitively, without the need for training, the participants did not receive an introductory training. Despite of that, 55.9 % of the participants could correctly perform the voice-based tasks on the first attempt, and 87.1 % of them succeeded by the third attempt. In the gesture condition, 64.8 % were successful in the first attempt and 91.6 % by the third. For a detailed discussion, see [10]. With the enhancements of the WISE platform a relaxed and peripheral, or *calm* interaction with a future home is possible, as depicted in Fig. 7.5.

Fig. 7.5 Screenshot of a video record of an interaction study [10] evaluating alternative interaction modalities (speech and gesture) for the interaction with the WISE platform. On the left-hand side a real-time view of the subject's mobile device screen is shown. On the right-hand side is the video in which the participant spontaneously lay down on the sofa to try out the functionality

7.2 Household 37: Bringing Technology Closer to Reality

After having developed the first release of the WISE platform and having conducted initial evaluations under lab conditions, the next logical step was to evaluate its suitability as a real-world installation. As we did not have living lab facilities that would allow participants to stay there for longer periods of time, the major question related to this attempt was where to install the platform. Several challenges and obstacles had to be considered. First, as [11] pointed out, average homes are generally not prepared for the types of devices that constitute a smart home system. There are specific problems and efforts in retrofitting [12], up to an even *tremendous* amount of overhead [13] that would accompany the establishment of a physical smart home test-bed. Expertise and resources are needed to design and install the sensors, controllers, network components, and middle-ware just to perform basic data collection [13]. According to [12] retrofitting existing dwellings is far more expensive and messy. For those reasons, it is easy to understand why only few physical test-beds exist. The second aspect to be considered is the privacy issues related to a potentially-permanent observation of the people living in the test-beds. Both aspects would have made it difficult or even impossible to deploy the system in the home of someone unrelated to our research activities. The deployment of technology *sounds good in theory, but proves to be very difficult in practice* [14]. This is probably also one reason why so many research activities are carried out in artificial environments instead of going into the field. Besides the efforts related to the initial installations, there are also the additional challenges of maintenance and administration of the installation. Research labs typically do have personnel for this task, but this is not natural in a private home. The pragmatic solution for the problem has been to establish the first real world test-bed in a house belonging to a member of the research team. Since I was the driving force behind this research, my house became the test-bed. It is not exceptional or even rare for researchers to conduct experiments in their own homes. According to [11] the same approach was followed in the adaptive home project and also in the pioneering work of Sutherland for the development of the Echo IV. The goal had to be to harmonize living and research, and prevent the impression of *living in a prototype* [15]. This was not always possible, but that also seems to be a trait experienced by other researchers [16].

Before being able to install the platform in a real household, we had to extend the architecture in order to enable a remote connection between the university servers that were responsible for a central data repository, and the remote household systems. The latter were designed to run a redundant local independently-functioning control and backup system in case of connection problems. Figure 7.6 is depicting the principal architecture. The advancements in the architecture were already oriented on future requirements (e.g. considering the accessibility, as available to the trusted persons involved in the Casa Vecchia project, described later in this chapter).

Because of the necessity to ensure privacy, the identification of the field installations was based on code numbers. In order to ease further data analyses, incremental numbers were used to differentiate the households and their expansion

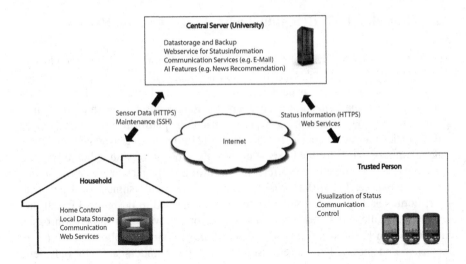

Fig. 7.6 Schema of the distributed architecture, consisting of the household installations, a central backup repository and data analysis platform at the university and a connection to external systems and users

stages. The higher the numbers, the more mature the stages of expansion. This system was responsible for the first field test-bed receiving the codename household 37 (HH37).

The final increment, shown in Fig. 7.7 includes 60 sensors and actuators + infrastructural components such as a server running the WISE platform.

Because of the close relationship between the researchers and HH37, this test bed cannot be considered a pure field installation, but must be treated as an interstage between a living lab and real world deployment. The research performed can be considered a participant-observer-designer approach [11], which means that the researcher has different roles which have to be managed very carefully. These kinds of methods have a long tradition in sociology and psychology, for example in the concept of participant observation [17]. The researcher is not only observing the topic of research from outside, but is himself an integral part of the research context. This has advantages and disadvantages. The advantage is that the natural behaviour of the other persons can be assumed not to be influenced by the presence of the researcher. The disadvantage is the lack of objectivity of the results achieved. HH37 had many different purposes but can generally be seen as a longitudinal case study with the goal of evaluating the technical feasibility and further development of the WISE platform. However it also became possible to evaluate socio-psychological aspects, as shown in the multi-user example later in this section. The experiences that could be gained over the course of almost ten years of investigation provided valuable insights and inputs for the further development and preparation of the platform to be used in other projects. This was especially true for the Casa Vecchia project. On the technological level, one aspect has been of major importance. Household 37 turned out to be extremely useful for applied research in the smart

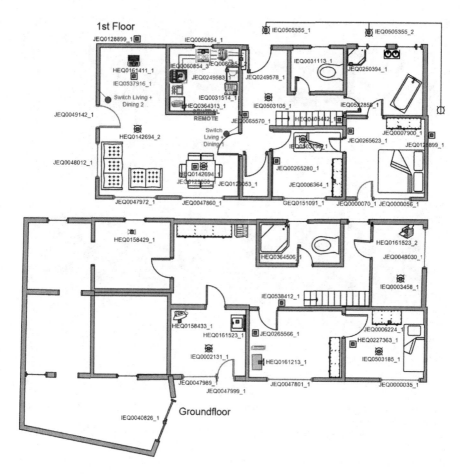

Fig. 7.7 Floorplan of Household 37 showing the latest increment of the smart home platform and positions of sensors and actuators

home field, helping to achieve results on very diverse levels, some of which are illustrated in this section.

The first example shows the problems of deploying smart home systems in real world settings on the one hand, but also shows progress on the other. HH37 was, like the lab facilities, equipped with smart components of the first generation hardware platform. As in the lab, a few years later the components in HH37 were also superseded components of the new hardware platform, because of the technical shortcomings mentioned earlier. Figure 7.8 illustrates the problems related to the retrofit of smart technology in an average home, as discussed in the related literature. The integration of components of the initial hardware platform for the roller blinds, for example, required demolition work which would probably have caused a heart attack in the inhabitants of other households. Over the years, as

Fig. 7.8 The figure shows the changes in component size between the first installation on the *top* and the second version on the *bottom*

illustrated by the lower picture showing the components of the new hardware platform, miniaturization brought smaller form factors, which made components fit into standard junction boxes.

However, as the examples of installation work in Fig. 7.9 show, we are far from having systems that can be technically integrated in a smooth manner into an average home.

Another example from the context of HH37 shows the possibilities to address societal big challenges with smart home components; more concretely, the problem of wasted energy. A side effect of the installation of smart components in household 37 was the ability to observe the power consumption status of devices, though, at first, this could only be done manually. The reasons my family and I accepted the demolition work[2] were that my family supported my intrinsic interest in the research, and that we live in an old house. We had to do some refurbishing

---

[2] At this point I have to do two thing. First, to apologize for the troubles that my experiments has caused to them and, second, to say thank you a thousand times to the three women who share my life.

Fig. 7.9 A selection of smart home components that have been installed. On the *left*, an actuator controlling outside lights is shown. In the *middle*, components in the fusebox observing the status of attached devices (e.g. kitchen stove), on the *right*, a sensor that is tracking a water consumption

anyway, and were optimistic that the amount of additional installations necessary for the research would not matter much. Independently from the research goal we were concerned about our energy consumption. We had assumed, along with several experts, that our high energy consumption was due to the fact that the house was not thermally insulated. Sequentially, new windows were installed and some other measures were taken to increase energy efficiency, but according to the information we had, consumption would only decrease significantly once the house was fully thermally insulated. This thermal insulation took place in 2012. The consumption of electric energy dropped around 20 %, but not to the degree we had expected. The energy consumption was still above the consumption of an average, 4-person household. Being sceptical about that consumption rate, and with the smart installations that were now available, I began to investigate the situation. What I found was quite surprising. One of the results of consulting with experts, as mentioned earlier, was that none of the devices present in our home were outdated; meaning that none of them could be unequivocally identified as uniquely responsible for the high energy consumption. This was also the situation after the insulation. All of the devices seemed to be working as intended, and would not waste more energy than needed. The basic problem was a problem of regulation in the heating system that involved the three components shown in Fig. 7.10. Our home uses a wood stove as primary energy source for heating. There is also a solar thermal system which serves as a support system. The heating and the hot water for both personal hygiene and domestic purposes are stored in a combined water buffer. As a backup system, an electrical heating cartridge is installed in the buffer to make sure that the temperature of the water used for domestic water does not fall below a predefined threshold. The reason for the high energy consumption was related to one of the central laws of thermodynamics: corresponding vessels strive for thermal equilibrium. In our case, because of mistakes in the routing of the water piping

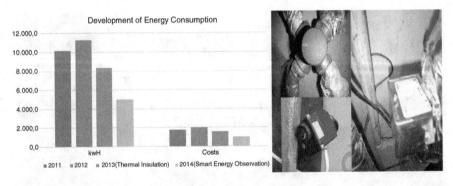

Fig. 7.10   Development of energy costs and the "responsible" components

systems, the hot water in the system was not running past the electrical heating cartridge. Instead, the cartridge was being bathed in cold water, which signalled that the water temperature had fallen below the threshold and constantly needed electrical heating. This problem could not be identified by single measurements but by observing the situation and its development for a longer period of time. With the identification of this problem and its correction, alongwith a few more minor problems, it was possible to reduce energy consumption by another 30 %. The data is presented in Fig. 7.10, as well as the components which were responsible for the problem. The numbers can be verified with energy bills (although this would be a little embarrassing).

The reduction in energy consumption and costs cannot be sold as an unqualified success. Compared to the demands of what a WISE home system should be, the success of the project was only relative. The search for causes, and the recording, measurement and comparison all had to be done manually, which was complex and cumbersome. It produced efforts which would probably not have been in the interest (or within the ability) of average consumers. Obviously, problems do not only occur in regards to the control of smart homes. There are also drawbacks in the observation of operational status. This aspect motivated other research work, the findings of which managed to piece together another piece of the jigsaw of the WISE home of the future. My colleague AJ Fercher [18] analysed the possibilities of energy visualization, in relation to calmness. As pointed out in Chap. 2 devices in a conventional home typically try to compete for the (focussed) attention of the user. But information could also be provided in a reserved and decent way, such as illustrated in the work of [19]. The display of information about energy consumption provides a good example for this. It should be possible to observe energy consumption peripherally, reserving the ability to intervene if necessary, but without any demand for care or concern. The solution shown in Fig. 7.11 is based on the concept of informative art [20] and includes elements of the concept *perceivable energy* [18]. The plant on coffee table illustrates the current level of energy consumption. When the plant is in good shape, this means that the energy consumption is in an average range. A wilting plant shows that energy consumption

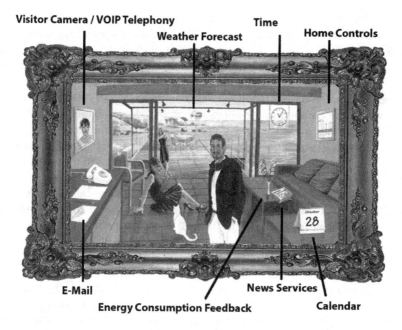

Visitor Camera / VOIP Telephony   **Time**

Weather Forecast   **Home Controls**

E-Mail   **News Services**

Energy Consumption Feedback   **Calendar**

Fig. 7.11 Information Visualisation in a calm way, based on an artwork of A. Fercher (used with permission). The artwork was used in the Casa Vecchia project (described in detail in Sect. 7.3) as the interface of the central unit. Beside other features, it shows the current level of energy consumption. If the plant on the living room table is in good condition, this symbolizes an appropriate level of energy consumption. If the plant is wilted, this shows that too much energy is consumed and symbolizes environmental degradation [18]

is too high, having a negative impact on the environment. Figure 7.11 shows the central interface of the Casa Vecchia project and includes additional functionality. The design represents only one example of energy visualization, other alternatives are depicted in [18]. People could decide the motif for displaying their energy consumption themselves. The interface does not only allow the observation of the current level of energy consumption, but also, for example, a comparison with historical data.

The research presented next was carried out in HH37 with a focus on the recognition of activity patterns of multiple users [21, 22]. For this purpose approximately 500,000 separate pieces of sensor data have been collected over the last two years. The series of studies had the goal of being able to differentiate between the activities of the inhabitants just on the basis of smart home components and observation of individual sequences of activity. The study was carried out in cooperation with [21]. Illustrations of preliminary results are shown below. As pointed out above, within these settings there was a danger of confounding the roles of the different people involved (researcher vs. observed object). In the starting phases this problem was overcome by qualitative observations of the interactions between the installed system and those inhabitants who were not involved in the research. One of the first questions addressed has been if and how the other members of the family are using or accepting smart home functionality. The results were that some of the functions were appreciated. The remote control to close or open the blinds with only one button press was frequently used, specifically in the living room, as shown on the charts that are depicted on the left hand side of Fig. 7.14. The problem was the different modes. Pressing buttons longer activated a different function – programming the duration of the blinds to go up or down. These different modes were difficult to understand and led to involuntary re-programming of components. On a subjective level, the smart home installations and studying their behaviour had the effect that the family members were scared of the installations and had the feeling of being permanently observed (Fig. 7.12).

The studies conducted in later stages strictly separate the inhabitants actively and passively collecting the data from the researcher conducting the analyses (who is not resident in HH37) [21]. The goal of a recent multi-user study was to develop unsupervised learning algorithms that would be able to identify behavioural patterns (in the sense of implicit interaction, as described in Sect. 5.1.2) and to derive individualized automated functionality with the enhanced difficulty of differentiating between the inhabitants. Behavioural patterns had to be learned by the system during the training and evaluation stage. This required additional sources of information (in the form of annotations) in order to achieve *ground truths* as a basis for machine learning; to extract data noise; and to separate activity patterns from different users which the system might have combined by mistake. Annotation methods included diary-keeping with a spreadsheet and with a mobile app, enabling the users to protocol their activities based on icons which had to be pressed when an activity started and again when it ended. The final tool to annotate activities was based on smart cameras, which periodically shot photos of the contexts the users were in. Figure 7.13 depicts some of the impressions from the viewpoint of the persons wearing the camera. Figure 7.14 provides an interesting insight into the progress of research over the last few years. Beside the establishment of the technical infrastructure enabling field-based smart home research, much effort was applied in the first years of research to the development of tools that support evaluations *in the wild*, as described in detail in [23–25]. When the attempt to develop tools to support field research started, we had to develop our own systems supporting these contextual evaluations. Meanwhile, as shown in the lower part of Fig. 7.14, integrated systems (e.g. Autographer[3]) have come into being and the possibilities of data combination and visualisation have improved [21].

The final example of HH37 demonstrates the relationships between smart technology and complex constructs that drive life at home. If the technology is appropriate, it does not give rise to conflicts with the values of the intended user. This is shown by the small example of the switch depicted in Fig. 7.15. In my younger daughter's bedroom, the light switches are positioned beside the entrance doors, as is quite common in houses of a certain age. This is a disadvantage when one

---

[3]http://www.autographer.com/

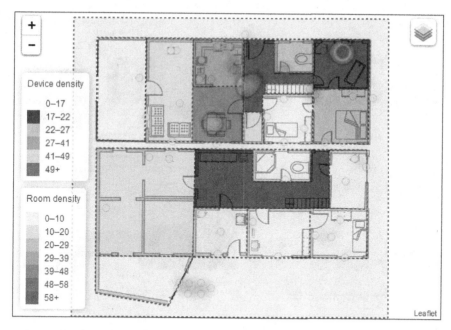

Fig. 7.12 Business in different rooms in the morning

Fig. 7.13 Scenes recorded with the necklace camera Autographer which periodically shoots pictures from the perspective of the user who wears it

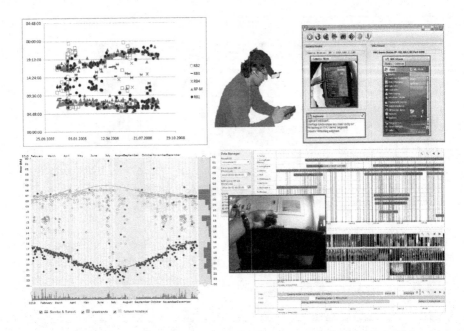

Fig. 7.14 Multiuser tracking and pattern analysis, in the *upper part* the initial, custom made, status and in the *lower part* the current systems in use [21]

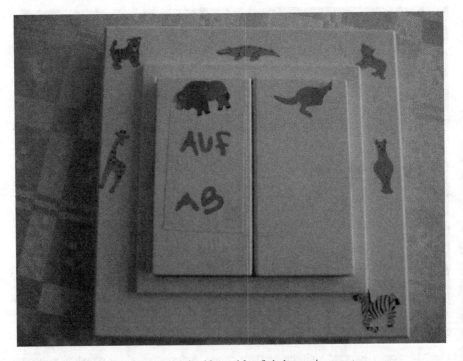

Fig. 7.15 Switch that has been customized by a girl to fit in her environment

would like to turn the lights on or off from some other location. For example, the bed is often located in the middle of the room, where no light switch is available. The conventional approach to solving this problem would be to do demoliton work, and install new wires and a wired switch near the bed. This would be cumbersome and it would also be anachronistic. If the bed were moved, then the position from which the lights are switched would have to be changed again, and the entire rewiring procedure would have to be repeated. As HH37 is fully equipped with smart components, another solution would have been to provide control for the lights. The problem that could be observed specifically with the children in the household was that they had some difficulties in mentally mapping different devices to the different buttons of the remote control. The preferred solution was therefore to install a wall mounted but smart switch right above my daughter's bed. The switch had two rockers and we could therefore not only enable switching lights but also the blinds, the original switch of which was near the window. The smart switch seemed to work, but it turned out that it was not as un-intrusive and intuitive as expected. One day my daughter asked me if she was allowed to re-design the switch a little bit. I did not know what she meant by that, but allowed it. The result is shown in Fig. 7.15. When asking her about her motivation she told me that the blank white switch seemed to her to be too out-of-place between her cuddly toys. It also occurred to me that, since she was not able to read at that time, the animal stickers on the switch served as memory aids, reminding her of the meanings of the different rocker positions. For example, the kangaroo jumps up, and therefore rocking the switch towards the kangaroo means that the blinds go up, too.

Although the experiences gained with HH37 are idiosyncratic and not representative, they proved to be of great help in the follow-up projects that were based on field deployment. Remember the German colleague who admitted that he would not want to live in his living lab? Many other researchers do not have the long-term experience of living in a smart home and so cannot use this experience to estimate, understand and solve problems that can occur in projects. Some of our experiences were interesting in terms of application to research, while many others served only to point out the boring reality of day-to-day life at home. In terms of installation and maintenance the work in HH37 was sometimes quite cumbersome. Sometimes that seemed understandable, others not. The troubles with the first installation was very annoying. Quite often it occurred that the system did not work, but because of the complexity of the system (gateway, PC, drivers, software components), searching for the problem was fatiguing. Fortunately, this changed with the new platform, where all mechanics and the control software were concentrated in one device. The weakest components in all stages of expansion were the batteries. In the context of studying activity patterns, some of them had to be exchanged preventively on a weekly basis. Components such as door contacts were very sensible for slamming doors, not maliciously, but simply as a typical way to close them. The door sensors stopped working because batteries became dislocated. But as was demonstrated with the generational changes of the roller blind actuators in Fig. 7.8, this problem has since been solved by components which integrate solar cells that produce enough energy to keep them operational for years. Other components, such as smart switches, can store the kinetic energy that is produced by pushing the rocker to load the battery. The experiences and results that could be gained in a setting such as HH37 could not have been achieved elsewhere, specifically in terms of be of realism of the collected data. The research itself brought interesting insights, specifically on the qualitative level.

7.3 Active and Assisted Living: The Casa Vecchia Project

The project presented in this section illustrates an attempt to overcome the limitations of lab experiments on the one hand, and the idiosyncratic perspective of a case study on the other. Experimental research has the benefit of objective and quantitative data, but the outcome often lacks external validity, due to the artificiality of the setting. A case study based on participant observation is biased by idiosyncratic and subjective elements and therefore the generalizability is questionable. In response to these issues, we designed a research project to combine the benefits and overcome the shortcomings of both types of study. The WISE platform was used as the basis of a possible solution to the difficulties involved in using Ambient Assisted Living (AAL), a concept which was recently renamed into Active and Assisted living, which is, in my opinion, emphasizes the goal to achieve in a much better way. The goal of the project was to address the threats of an ageing population, within the specific contextual conditions. AAL is based on the idea of applying any technology to support the elderly in their living contexts and to enable them to stay for a prolonged period within their *own four walls*. If any technology can be applied, then smart home technology should be applicable, too. With the help of appropriate technology, the elderly should be able to lead an independent life and to stay in their accustomed homes longer and in an enhanced quality than would be possible without such technology. Numerous AAL projects have been carried out all over the world during the course of the last decade. For examples of an overview see [26, 27]. Promising results were achieved, but a significant percentage of those projects followed the approach of moving elderly people into newly-built or refurbished care facilities equipped with AAL technology. Within these settings [12] only see marginal benefits of technology. Many surveys show that the majority of seniors want to stay at home in their old age [28]. In consideration of the proverb which exists in many languages: *"You cannot move an old tree without it dying"*, the goal of our attempt was to bring appropriate technology to the people and not the other way around. Relocating the elderly can have dramatic consequences. Statistics show that the majority of people moved to nursing homes die within the first 6 months [29]. The reasons can be manifold, but probably are strongly related to the fact that people lose their feeling of being home, their familiarity with the environment, and confidence in their own abilities. Taking into consideration the meaning a home could have, which could only be superficially touched in Chap. 3, the consequences are understandable. I recently heard a sad story from a friend who knew about my work and was interested in using the WISE platform for her grandmother. However, because of the grandmother's condition and her living circumstances, it was not possible to support her with our solution. Although the grandmother in question was over 90 years old at the time, she still was able to manage her household, cook meals, independently manage her personal hygiene, and dress herself. She was supported by the family, who arranged frequent phone calls and at least two personal visits per day. The main responsible person was her son, but when he became sick and had to move into a hospital, his mother had also to be moved to a nursing home. My friend described the vast problems that her grandmother had in adjusting to her new living situation. For example, when she woke up at night and wanted to go to the bathroom, she stumbled or knocked things over as she felt her way in the dark. Clearly this happened because she was not familiar with the environment and was disoriented. This loss of familiarity had a deep impact on her. She passed away shortly after being transferred to the nursing home.

One of the central goals of *Casa Vecchia* was to protect the elderly from such dramatic experiences. Casa Vecchia is the Italian translation for *old house* and the name should emphasize the intentions of the approach; retrofitting new technology into *old houses* to enable an enhanced quality of life. This constituted an optimal way to approve the concept for the WISE home idea, the flexibility and adaptability of the platform and the process model described in Chaps. 5 and 6. The experiences and results that we could achieve in our lab experiments and in the context of HH37 built the basis for the project. Because of the inherent flexibility of the approach we could take into account the ample literature and resources available in the smart home field in general and in the AAL field in particular. We could easily integrate methods, concepts and software components without having to re-examine the whole development cycle from lab, model homes, field deployments. Instead we were able to integrate results directly with little effort [30].

Besides the main focus of the project on bringing AAL technologies to the ancestral homes of the elderly, the secondary focus of Casa Vecchia was to bring that technology to rural areas. The central methodological goal, field deployment and research of the WISE platform had to correspond to the availability of opportunities. Carinthia, Austria where our research institution is located is mainly made up of rural areas with only a few small to middle-sized cities. But this was not the only reason to focus on rural areas. Rural areas have a high socio-political relevance, because a significant percentage of the world's population lives in rural areas. Speaking from the EU member states, for example, this means that 125 million people live in rural areas, which is about 25 % of the entire population of the European Union [31, 32]. In terms of topography rural areas even represent around 80 % of the territory of Europe. Although the concrete numbers differ from country to country and from region to region, the relevance of rural areas can be considered comparable all over the world. Rural areas will play a specific role in the context of the big societal challenges in the future. Demographic change will have a higher impact on those areas, because phenomena such as rural escape have seen to it that rural areas are already currently characterised by a disproportionately high percentage of the elderly. In regards to economic developments to increase efficiency and reduce costs, rural areas will probably suffer to a higher extent from savings in infrastructure and supplies. People who need increased support, such as the elderly, would be disadvantaged by such developments if no countermeasures are taken. As has been already demonstrated in the past, technology can help to compensate for the consequences of such developments, if it is appropriately designed. A central goal of the WISE approach followed in the Casa Vecchia project was therefore to design supporting technology in a WISE way. The technology should not overrule and overexert people by turning their lives upside down, but enhance and strengthen their existing way of life with technology only where this is appropriate. It was therefore of high importance to carefully analyse not only the immediate living circumstances of the elderly but to additionally involve their social network, and local organizations and craftsmen. This was realized by involving a *trusted person*, a relative, neighbour or friend, together with each elderly person that participated in the project.

One problem related to the dissemination of home technology emphasized in the earlier chapters of this book was the understandable reluctance of average end consumers to adopt such technology into their homes, and to adapt to it once it was there. The relevance of this problem was also confirmed during the Casa Vecchia participant acquisition phase. The target group for the project, elderly people living at home in the region of Carinthia, constitutes around 50,000 people. The prerequisites to participate in the project were that the seniors were living independently and did not require professional support or permanent care. No knowledge in handling computers was required. Although we used channels for advertising the project such as popular newspapers and local radio stations, which are known to have a high penetration among the target group, only around one thousandths of the target group responded to our announcements. Some of the people who contacted us had to be excluded because of incorrect expectations about the project, or because of their being in a status (e.g. in a health condition) which would not have made possible to participate for ethical or security reasons. Of course we do not know the exact motives of the more than 49,000 people who did not contact us,but we did get feedback from around 200 elderly people in the course of senior days where we presented the project. Additionally a questionnaire survey was carried out addressing nursing and healthcare personnel. About 150 completed questionnaires were returned to us. The outcome of both evaluations was, in summary, a strong fear of having to install complicated technology in the home and becoming dependent on it, or even being at its mercy. Bad experiences with, and ignorance of, technology were obviously the biggest hindrances to potential participants. This hypothesis was confirmed by the characteristics of the persons who finally participated in the project. All of the participants had previous experiences with computers and therefore seemed to be kind of open to new technologies or at least less reluctant than the majority. The range of computer literacy in the sample was broad. One elderly woman, for example, had an outdated PC on which she only played solitaire from time to time. The other extreme was an elderly woman who told us that she had some experiences with computers but did not consider herself a knowledgeable computer user. During one of our first meetings she showed us her favourite video on YouTube and informed us that she frequently does Skype calls with her grandson who was currently on study stay in Australia. Between these two extremes, we also found every level of computer literacy, and many examples of computer usage for very specific purposes (e.g. to arrange the instrumentation of musical pieces). Although the general access to technology in the group of participants was positive, this did not mean that they were naïve in this regard. They also expressed concerns in regards to the technology, for example, the *youtube woman* was concerned about increased electronic smog caused by wireless technology. Other participants mentioned their concerns in regards to data collection and privacy.

Although the participants had a certain similarity in regards to their experience with computers, they were very different on other characteristics. The spectrum of former professions, for example, ranged from farmers, workers, and drivers, to nurses, entrepreneurs, and managers. Their level of education was generally higher than in the average population. Occasionally persons of lower social classes were interested in the project. In one case a retired lady being dependent on a wheelchair would have been interested in participating in the project but, in the end, she and her family were too sceptical about the real intentions of these scientists (us) and about what they might really be asked or tricked into doing. Such misunderstandings did not only occur with members of low societal class. A retired medical doctor, who was obviously a very prosperous member of the upper class, had a completely false impression of how we might conduct our research, and to what end. He wanted the smart home equipment, support and maintenance for free, but with no balancing contribution from his side; no participating in interviews, no allowing data collection, and no filling in of questionnaires.

It was only later in the project that we came to realize that there was another, probably more important, similarity in the motivation of the participants that finally stayed in the project. All of them had direct or indirect past experiences with severe health problems. The range of experiences were broad, and included problems with one's own personal health – such as heart attacks and strokes, or other severe problems that had to be treated with complex surgeries. Others were motivated to participate by indirect experiences such as observing the beginning cognitive impairments in their partner or being responsible for care-dependent relatives. In the interviews all participants had expressed the fear that sooner or later they would have to leave their current home if their own health conditions or the condition of their partner should change. However, if and when this would happen was unclear and unforeseeable, and this uncertainty was a burden to them. They therefore welcomed any research on technology that could provide security and support features-hoping for alternatives to moving into nursing homes. Moving into a nursing home was not seen as a *natural* option in the rural areas, in which the majority of the Casa Vecchia participants were living. The topographic distribution of the participating households is shown in Fig. 7.16

About half of the persons participating in Casa Vecchia were elderly singles, the other half of them were living in a partnership. The majority of trusted persons involved in the project were adult children or other relatives. In single cases they

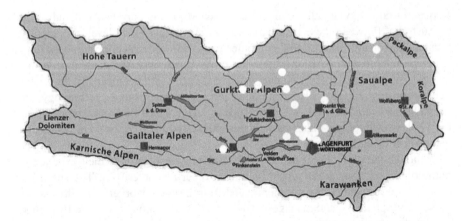

Fig. 7.16 Topographic distribution of participating households. The *white circles* represent the participating households. The *blue rectangles* represent the bigger cities in Carinthia (ranging between 10,000 and 60,000 inhabitants); the polygon shows the location of the university (where the server infrastructure is hosted) in the capital of Carinthia (which has around 100,000 inhabitants [30])

were neighbours or close friends. Details on the demographic data, taken from [30], can be found in Table 7.1.

Concrete AAL functionality had to be designed and developed in order to achieve Casa Vecchia's goals to support the elderly in staying in their own homes in old age. Two categories of functions were developed which correspond to what the related literature identified as the most important needs to be supported with AAL. The first was to enhance the security of the elderly. Due to the fact that elderly people are, with an increasing probability, living alone and – in our case – additionally in remote areas, we investigated possible ways in which technology could enhance their security. Also based on the consideration of bridging distances to the outside world, the second category of functions had the goal of enhancing the variety and quality of communication.

One of the major challenges in the preparatory work for Casa Vecchia involved the technical installations. Given the experiences with HH37 these difficulties were kind of expected. Our approach had to bear in mind the potential but understandable fear of being overruled by technology on the one hand and Mark Weiser's idea of unobtrusive and *disappearing* technology on the other. The consequences were that we installed the components of our system in a way that it did not influence the existing infrastructure and devices but that, rather, worked in parallel to them. If the smart system did not work in the expected way, the conventional components were still operational. As a second important feature the system was optimized to provide the highest possible level of stability and self-healing functionality. This meant, for example, that after a power outage (which frequently happened, specifically in remote areas) the system rebooted itself automatically. Achieving those features was not an easy task because of the vast range of households participating in the project,

Table 7.1 Overview on the demographic characteristics of the Casa Vecchia sample

Age	Gender	Persons in household	Marital status	Former profession	Trusted person
73	m	1	Widowed	Worker, farmer	Son
62	f	2	Married	Hairdresser, housewife	Son
64	f	2	Married	Nurse, office clerk	Daughter
64	f	2	Married	Translator	Partner
66	m	2	Partnership	Social insurance clerk	Son
73	f	1	Widowed	Teacher	Son
64	m	2	Married	Kindergarden nurse	Neighbour
50	f	2	Married	Branch manager, clothing	Partner
71	m	2	Married	Mechanical engineer	Son
63	f	2	Married	Primary school teacher	Daughter in law
69	m	2	Married	Company owner, consultant	Son
66	f	1	Divorced	Nurse	Daughter
60	m	2	Married	Company car driver	Neighbour
61	f	2	Married	Hospital manager	Neighbour
70	f	1	Widowed	Hospitality industry	Son
71	f	1	Widowed	Owner of transport company	Sister
62	f	1	Widowed	School janitor	Daughter
64	m	2	Married	Highschool teacher	Sister
67	f	1	Widowed	Office clerk	Daughter, grandson
69	f	1	Divorced	Support for crime victims	Daughter
70	m	2	Married	M.D.	Partner
83	f	1	Widowed	Office clerk	Daughter

Mean Age 66,45
Age Standard Deviation 6,39
Main Persons in Project
Female: 14
Male: 8
Sample size Main Persons: 22
Sample size with Partners 35
(without Trusted Persons)

in terms of their age and their infrastructure. We installed our system into a 300 year old farm house, into several detached family homes from the second half of the twentieth century, into apartments being part of a bigger electrical infrastructure, and into a low energy house which already had a highly-sophisticated technical system for heating and climate, but no other smart features. We were even able to install and run the WISE platform in a completely energy autarchic farmhouse in which all electricity was supplied by photo-voltaics.

Fig. 7.17 Smart phone of trusted person with different background colors and alerting signals (Picture taken form [30])

To support the first category of AAL features – to enhance the security of the elderly – a selection of different solutions was developed corresponding to the two major forms of interaction provided by the WISE platform: *implicit interaction* and *explicit interaction*. As pointed out in Chap. 5, implicit interaction is based on artificial intelligence (AI). In the Casa Vecchia project AI supported the observation of the activity of participants and to determine whether or not an activity was regular [30]. If the activity deviated significantly from the norm, the system could automatically trigger an alarm to the outside world. Typically, this alarm was used to signal the trusted person who had previously been assigned to the role by the participant. According to the experiences that were learned from other projects [33], devices that have to be triggered manually or worn on the body have a high level of errors. Our approach was fully based on environmental sensors and actuators and, because it did not depend on explicit triggers, can be seen as a form of calm or peripheral interaction. The signals of deviating behaviour were sent to the trusted person's smart phone, as shown in Fig. 7.17. If a certain threshold was exceeded, the background of the smart phone (based on a traffic light metaphor) turned from green to yellow. If the probability that an incident had occurred was high, the background of the smart phone turned to red and the phone also sent acoustic signals.

The integration of potentially dangerous devices such as the kitchen stove into the WISE platform was another way to enhance the security of the elderly participants. The basic problem which could necessitate an intervention in this regard is the increased probability of forgetting things with age. The stove has the potential to be one of the most dangerous devices in an average household. It is responsible for a high percentage of burn accidents [34]. The technology-oriented approach (which is represented by products available on the market) would be to install an additional device, typically consisting of a switch coupled to a timer which has to be pre-programmed. If a person wants to cook, she or he has to press the additional switch or to activate the timer. Although these systems have advantages in terms of enhancing security, they bear several problems. It is difficult specifically for the elderly to change procedures they have been familiar with for a long time. Adding steps or components to a procedure could lead to a discontinuation of routines. This contradicts the demand to keep the elderly mentally fit, to support their independence and their dignity. The WISE approach we followed was therefore not to install a hurdle in the path of familiar interaction with familiar devices, but to try to enhance security in another way. The result was a custom component in the fuse box of the household coupled with a smoke detector. The usage of the kitchen stove stayed as it was before installing the smart components. But the automatic coupling with the smoke detector enhanced the security of the participants without interfering in their behaviour, and without the need for additional programming. I have to admit that our approach also had some drawbacks. For example, there were some false alarms. When people cooked pasta and poured the hot water in the sink, the steam was sometimes detected by the smoke detector, which immediately shut off the stove. However, this showed that our intervention did work. The difference in the approach is small but important. The additional switch might represent the easiest technological solution, installing a security level on the interface between the user and the technical system. The WISE approach is to leave the interface as it was, because it is familiar to the user. The security level is not put on the interface between user and the system, but in the back-end of the technical system.

Another security feature we tried to provide shows the limitations of current smart home system components. With the same type of switches that was depicted in Fig. 7.15 we tried to provide a central point of control for the enhancement of security. We installed a smart switch on the entrance door of the participating households in order to fulfil several purposes. First, the switch should prevent the system from triggering false alarms. When people left their homes they should press the switch to inform the system that they are not at home, so perceived deviations from regular activity patterns should not trigger an alarm. Second, all potentially dangerous devices such as the kitchen stove, a socket plug for the iron, and other hazards are automatically disconnected from the power mains. The final benefit was that when the system was aware of the absence of residents, it could simulate their presence in order to scare away potential burglars. The advantage of such a WISE presence simulation, in comparison to simple timer based solutions, would be that algorithms based on AI can use a random generator for the simulation and this would make it harder for somebody observing a scene to find regularities. However, despite of all of our intentions, the switch did not meet our expectations, because it did not fulfil the fundamental requirements that devices from an HCI perspective should have. As emphasized in Chap. 2 these are, for example, appropriate feedback, mapping, and affordances (signifiers). The switch was smart because it didn't have to be connected to the wiring of the household and therefore could be put anywhere. This advantage has a drawback, which is the energy supply. To be able to design such a switch in a slim and attractive form, only a small battery can be placed inside. In order not to have to change the battery often, energy consumption has to be reduced. Switches of the first series solved this problem by not providing any feedback at all (such as an LED flashing when the switch was triggered). A typical feedback mechanism from conventional switches was missing too, which is the position of the rocker. I know many people who could tell the status of an attached device based on the position of the rocker of the switch. Unfortunately, the smart switches which are part of many smart home systems have only a single resting state. Rocking the switch sends a binary actuation or deactivation impulse to the system. But the rocker does not stay in a position that might be used as a visual sign of whether the device is on or off. Instead, it always moves back to the original position so as not to continue sending a stream of impulses to the system. The result was that this switch had the same problems that had been criticised about technically oriented solutions. People did not integrate it into their *mental model* of the home and, because of missing feedback mechanisms, the switch did not remind them of its functionality. The reason to describe this problem at this point is to show that even the smallest details can have a high relevance and impact, and, such real-world insights could never be achieved in artificial settings or under lab conditions.

The other type of functionality provided in Casa Vecchia was communication features. The function to inform the trusted persons via their smart phones about the status of the elderly they care for is kind of a mixture between security and communication function. The other functionalities we provided had the focus of providing easier access to features of the Internet. As mentioned earlier, all of the participants had some experience with computers and some of them, such as the *youtube woman* did not need to be supported in their communication with new media. For the others, such as the woman who had only used her computer to play solitaire, we thought about how to provide the benefits of improved communication, but in a WISE approach focusing on their needs rather than on the technical possibilities. This required a change of perspective and a deconstruction of the state-of-the-art. Consider, for example, current E-Mail functionality. A frequent computer user is familiar with the steps involved in writing an E-Mail. Before being able to do that, they have to overcome the hurdles of the operating system such as logging in and selecting the appropriate E-Mail client program. The structure of a conventional E-Mail client program is complex. Many things have to be selected and defined, which make sense in formal correspondence, but maybe not in informal communication. Whoever remembers the time when we wrote paper letters and physically brought them to the letter box, probably also remembers the structure of the letters. Did anyone ever write a *subject header* on the birthday greetings for grandma? The approach that we followed was to throw away all the unnecessary stuff that should not bother a computer layperson and thus reduce the concept to what [35] would have called a *minimalist design*. Due to our team's knowledge and skills in regards to alternative interface concepts such as informative art [18, 20], we designed the E-Mail interface as a symbolic chalkboard where the participants could

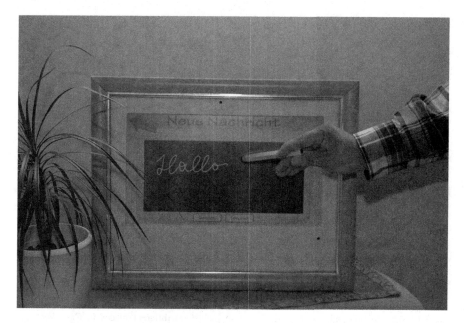

Fig. 7.18 Picture of the simplified E-Mail client

directly write notes on the touch display of the central unit depicted in Fig. 7.11 and send them to the preprogrammed E-mail address of either the trusted person they had previously identified, or of others they would like. With the possibility to carefully approach technology without being overwhelmed by it we could awake the interest in some participants to do more (Fig. 7.18).

Combined with the attempt to provide appropriate functionality to the people it was also a goal to deploy the technology used for communication and information purposes in a similarly unobtrusive form as the security function. However, those features are based on *explicit interaction* and insofar they required appropriate interfaces and devices to interact with. What we tried for several reasons was to design them in a way that they are not in the foreground and integrate them into the environment (in the sense of Weiser). Figure 7.19 shows examples of the positioning of the central units that provide those functionalities.

The previous discussion of Casa Vecchia may have drifted too far towards technical details and as a result, the difference between smart and WISE that has been addressed throughout the book may not yet be clear. But this is the reality. To be able to research the use of new technology it was necessary to conceptualize and install it. As pointed out in Chap. 5, we were only able to thoroughly investigate the potential impacts that the technology would have in the home once the infrastructure had been prepared. As was emphasized in Chap. 6, the real difference in the WISE approach, the difference that has hopefully also been demonstrated in the previous passages, is the variety of accompanying methods that can be applied in the phase of field deployments. In the course of Casa Vecchia, a mixture of methods was

Fig. 7.19 The central units of the WISE system placed on different places in Casa Vecchia households. As it is shown, the devices integrate themselves into the environments unobtrusively

applied – as described in detail in [30, 36]. In the following discussion, only a few examples of findings are provided. The investigations in Casa Vecchia started with interviews addressing the status of the potential participants and the trusted persons in regards to their living circumstances, their typical daily routines, their access to technology, and their social network. Based on this initial information the concrete installations of the WISE platform were conceptualized and customized to the individual circumstances. We built a customized evaluative instrument for the next phase of the project by combining aspects of three methodological concepts [37]. The central component of the approach was the technology acceptance model (TAM) [38]. The TAM has been used in numerous studies to investigate factors that are relevant to the use of technology, subsumed in the dimensions of *perceived ease of use* and *perceived usefulness*. These dimensions include many of the aspects that were presented in the theoretical parts of this book. For example, the motivation to show a behaviour is influenced by the self-assessment of being able to do so. The perceived ease of use dimension covers usability and user experience aspects of technologies. Perceived usefulness covers the utility of a technology, the purpose it fulfils. Other factors such as the subjective norm, considering the influence of relevant persons from the social network are also addressed. For our purposes, we adapted the TAM model to the home context and used it as a basis for the investigation of motivations and needs. The second central component of our evaluative instruments was the concept of contextual inquiry [39], focussing on the identification of relevant characteristics of the context within which a technology is used. Because the method had originally been developed for use in the context of work, it had to be adapted to the home context. The final concept included in our inventory is the social network analysis of [40].

In the course of four waves of evaluation, we collected information about the described dimensions and subsumed them into categories. The categories were:

- access to technology
- features of the social network
- life experiences and general life satisfaction
- demographic data and professional background, and
- private interests, engagement in associations, etc....

Combined with analyses of sensor data (in the course of the project we collected 2.5 million real-world datasets) we were able to form very interesting insights into what has to be done to make AAL technology a success. Details on the data analysis can be found in [21, 30], the following examples are intended to emphasise the ways in which situated research can be carried out in a WISE manner. It has been pointed out in Chap. 6 that a central element of an appropriate evaluation process is to *understand* the circumstances under which life takes place. This understanding can be achieved by observation, but this observation will be biased by the viewpoint and interpretation of the researcher. Our goal has been to find a more direct way of understanding what is important for our participants. Towards that end, we used the method of cultural probes [41]. We provided disposable cameras to our participants and asked them to take photos of situations and things that are important to them, things to which they have positive or negative associations, and other things they are immediately concerned with or about. In addition to written comments regarding the photographs, we asked the participants to put sticky notes on each scene, specifically writing things that would help us to categorize them. Sticky notes with a "+" on them meant that the situation is associated with positive thoughts, a "–" was telling us, that the situation had negative connotations. The colours of the sticky notes were also used to help us to associate the pictures to the different categories enumerated above. Because of the quality the disposable cameras provided, lighting conditions, and size of the photographs, the details are not as clear as we would have liked. The overall results that could be achieved from the cultural probes are that people enjoy being with family and friends, engage in activities such as playing cards or meeting in a choir. The majority of negative associations were related to technology. A washing machine, for example, supports important needs of hygiene, but is too complicated. The same applies to computers and mobile phones. Figure 7.20 includes a selection of the provided photographs.

Another methodological detail which might be considered to be kind of WISE was the way in which we recorded our interviews with the participants. It is typical that interview data should be digitized for the sake of efficiency and effectiveness. The problem is that devices to take notes such as laptops create a barrier between the interviewer and interviewee. Other technical devices such as smart phones, tablets or even dictaphones attract too much attention and disturb the setting. The alternative, conventional note taking, has the drawback that documents are available

Fig. 7.20 Cultural Probes – we gave disposable cameras to the participants and ask them to take photos from things in their lives that are relevant to them, in different categories. Relationship, Technology, Non-Technology, Happyness, etc. The photos can represent positive or negative aspects, or other aspects which we asked the participants to describe. The figure shows a snippet of the photos we got

in physical form, but then have to be digitized for the reasons referred to above. A nice technical solution (which is not an achievement of our own work, but is still kind of WISE despite that) is the system named Livescribe (TM). It consists of a notebook that looks like a conventional notebook and a pen which looks like a fairly conventional pen. The pen actually digitizes the writing in real time, and also captures an audio recording of the conversation. In this way the flow of communication is not disturbed by the obvious presence of technology. Everyone is used to a conversational partner who takes notes. The digitized contents are automatically generated and easily distributed within the team for further analyses.

The major insight from the project is that a WISE home system has to handle different requirements and motivations of the inhabitants on at least two different levels. Basic needs, such as those related to nutrition (representing lower levels of Maslow's needs hierarchy) have to be fulfilled without having to overcome additional obstacles. The elderly, but assumably also other users of smart technology, are not interested in pseudo-enhancements in the control of basic functionality, just in the end result. It should, for example, just be warm in the home, how this does happen it is not of interest. Interaction that is too complicated is not needed, nor is configuration. This would be an ideal area in which to apply the principles of implicit interaction based on AI features.

On the second level, it must be certain that interaction with the system is appropriate to the needs of the user. As [42] pointed out, things should become simpler in a smart home not more complicated. Additional remote controls to perform simple tasks are not appropriate. Other alternatives, such as speech interaction are therefore supported by the WISE platform. The example of the smart switch shows that many so-called smart devices are smart in terms of technology but do not appropriately meet basic requirements of interaction. Consider Weiser's [43] original idea that technology should convey all the necessary information to be used and not require *light switch literacy* [44].

As it could be observed in Casa Vecchia the use of technology is not continuous but undergoes phases. In the first phase of the project, when the technology was new and unknown, an euphoric contention with it was observable. This is not surprising and is, in fact, probable for all new things. When the technology became familiar, the quality and quantity of usage settled to a level which allowed a more realistic estimation of the acceptance of the technology and the influence it has on daily life. Although the goal to deploy the technology in an unobtrusive manner could be achieved to a reasonable extent, the technology still changed behaviour and effected interpersonal relationships, frequency and quality of contacts with people taking care of each other. A clear gender difference in regard to the access to technology was also observable. This is addressed in more detail in [36]. In short, men proved likely to be intrinsically motivated to use the technology, whereas women typically wanted to have functionality that would support them in overcoming concrete problems or limitations.

Another outcome that could probably not have been identified in laboratory settings is that there is not an overall level of acceptance and level of intrusion of the provided functionalities into daily life. Instead, there is a difference related to functionality. Life- and health-critical functionality should not – for several reasons – depend on explicit input from the user. First, in real emergency situations people may not be able to actively trigger an alarm. Therefore this kind of functionality should be automated. Second, active triggers based on a single device may lead to a higher probability of false alarms. With the possibility of interconnection provided by the WISE platform, the accuracy of differentiating between a real emergency situation and false positives can be enhanced by integrating the information of more than one sensor.

Third, a person in need may not be willing to trigger a call for help because, as we have heard in numerous interviews, they do not want to be a burden to their relatives or to generate unnecessary service costs (e.g. for professional care providers). This example has a clear relation to socio-psychological aspects, the value system of the respective persons which neither can be evaluated nor solved on a technical level alone. In contrast to that, people would not accept that a technical system automatically controls entertainment and communication features. These features require appropriate interfaces to enable and motivate users to use them frequently. Neither short term evaluations (conventional and periodical usability evaluations) would have discovered such phenomena, nor would short-term stays in living labs have been able to reveal the whole range of influential contextual aspects.

We could not have learned what we did over the course of the four years we spent accompanying our participants in their very own living circumstances, if we had had to rely on laboratory settings and short term investigations. For example, we would not have observed the different phases of highs and lows in the motivation of our participants. It was interesting to see how their attitude to technology changed – and not always in a positive way – once they understood what smart technology could and could not concretely do in their own environment. Some of the participants were quite disappointed with the limitations of the new technology, especially, for example, in regards to stability and reliability. Others were at once fascinated by and scared of the possibilities to track a person's activities and behaviour without having to fully equip him or her with a bunch of sensors, just by observing the usage of electric devices that just were intelligently coupled with smart home components.

References

1. Brush, A. J., Lee, B., Mahajan, R., Agarwal, S., Saroiu, S., & Dixon, C. (2011). Home automation in the wild: Challenges and opportunities. In *Proceedings of the SIGCHI Conference on Human Factors in Computing Systems* (pp. 2115–2124). New York: ACM.
2. Mennicken, S., & Huang, E. M. (2012). Hacking the natural habitat: An in-the-wild study of smart homes, their development, and the people who live in them. In *Pervasive computing* (pp. 143–160). Berlin/Heidelberg: Springer.
3. Felsing, D. (2009). *Eine erweiterbare Smart Home Plattform auf Basis des FS20 Systems*. Diploma Thesis, Alpen-Adria Universität Klagenfurt, Klagenfurt.
4. Samselnig, R. (2012). *Ein Smarthome lernt Ortsabhängigkeit*. Diploma Thesis, Alpen-Adria Universität Klagenfurt, Klagenfurt.

5. Florian, M. (2010). *Spielregeln zur Beherrschung von Konflikten zwischen Benutzerprofilen in Multiuser-Smart-Homes.* Diploma Thesis, Alpen-Adria Universität Klagenfurt, Klagenfurt.
6. Grötschnig, B. (2011). *Erkennung von Verhaltensmustern in Smart Homes zur Unterstützung älterer Menschen.* Diploma Thesis, Alpen-Adria Universität Klagenfurt, Klagenfurt.
7. Leitner, G., Fercher, A. J., & Lassen, C. (2013). End users programming smart homes – A case study on scenario programming. In *Human-computer interaction and knowledge discovery in complex, unstructured, big data* (pp. 217–236). Berlin/Heidelberg: Springer.
8. Lieberman, H., Paternò, F., Klann, M., & Wulf, V. (2006). *End-user development: An emerging paradigm* (pp. 1–8). Amsterdam: Springer.
9. Laugwitz, B., Held, T., & Schrepp, M. (2008). *Construction and evaluation of a user experience questionnaire* (pp. 63–76). Berlin/Heidelberg: Springer.
10. Brown, J. N. A. (2014). *Unifying interaction across distributed controls in a smart environment using anthropology-based computing to make human-computer interaction "Calm".* Ph.D. Thesis, Erasmus Mundus Doctorate Program in Interactive and Cognitive Environments (ICE), Alpen Adria Universität Klagenfurt.
11. Hindus, D. (1999). The importance of homes in technology research. In *Cooperative buildings. Integrating information, organizations, and architecture* (pp. 199–207). Berlin/Heidelberg: Springer.
12. Barlow, J., & Gann, D. (1998). A changing sense of place: Are integrated IT systems reshaping the home? http://139.184.32.141/Units/spru/publications/imprint/sewps/sewp18/sewp18.pdf.
13. Cook, D. J., & Schmitter-Edgecombe, M. (2009). Assessing the quality of activities in a smart environment. *Methods of Information in Medicine, 48*(5), 480.
14. Eckl, R., & MacWilliams, A. (2009). Smart home challenges and approaches to solve them: A practical industrial perspective. In *Intelligent interactive assistance and mobile multimedia computing* (pp. 119–130). Berlin/Heidelberg: Springer.
15. Takayama, L., Pantofaru, C., Robson, D., Soto, B., & Barry, M. (2012). Making technology homey: Finding sources of satisfaction and meaning in home automation. In *Proceedings of the 2012 ACM Conference on Ubiquitous Computing* (pp. 511–520). New York: ACM.
16. Horx, M. (2008). *Technolution: Wie unsere Zukunft sich entwickelt.* Frankfurt am Main: Campus.
17. Atkinson, P., & Hammersley, M. (1994). Ethnography and participant observation. In *Handbook of Qualitative Research* (Vol. 1(23), pp. 248–261). Thousand Oaks: Sage.
18. Fercher, A., Hitz, M., & Leitner, G. (2009). Pervasive approaches to awareness of energy consumption. In *Ami-Blocks*, Salzburg (pp. 3–8). Erlangen, Germany.
19. Weiser, M., & Brown, J. S. (1997). The coming age of calm technology. In *Beyond calculation* (pp. 75–85). New York: Springer.
20. Redström, J., Skog, T., & Hallnäs, L. (2000). Informative art: Using amplified artworks as information displays. In *Proceedings of DARE 2000 on Designing Augmented Reality Environments* (pp. 103–114). New York: ACM.
21. Ayuningtyas, C. *Activity modeling for multi-user environments.* Ph.D. Thesis. Erasmus Mundus Doctorate Program in Interactive and Cognitive Environments (ICE), Alpen Adria Universität Klagenfurt. Work in progress.
22. Leitner, G., Melcher, R., & Hitz, M. (2012). Spielregeln im intelligenten Wohnumfeld. In *Vernetzung als soziales und technisches Paradigma* (pp. 189–206). Wiesbaden: Springer VS.
23. Leitner, G., & Hitz, M. (2005). The usability observation cap. In *Proceedings of the 5th International Conference on Methods and Techniques in Behavioral Research* (pp. 8–13). Wageningen: Noldus.
24. Leitner, G., Plattner, S., & Hitz, M. (2006). Usability evaluation of mobile applications in leisure-oriented contexts. In *Information and communication technologies in tourism* (pp. 158–169). Vienna: Springer.
25. Leitner, G., Ahlström, D., & Hitz, M. (2007). Usability of mobile computing in emergency response systems: Lessons learned and future directions. In *HCI and usability for medicine and health care* (LNCS, Vol. 4799, pp. 241–254). Springer: Berlin/Heidelberg.

26. Chan, M., Estéve, D., Escriba, C., & Campo, E. (2008). A review of smart homes – Present state and future challenges. *Computer Methods and Programs in Biomedicine, 91*(1), 55–81.
27. Yamazaki, T. (2006). Beyond the smart home. In *International Conference on Hybrid Information Technology, 2006 (ICHIT'06)*, Cheju Island (Vol. 2, pp. 350–355). IEEE.
28. http://assets.aarp.org/rgcenter/general/home-community-services-10.pdf.
29. Kelly, A., Conell-Price, J., Covinsky, K., Cenzer, I. S., Chang, A., Boscardin, W. J., & Smith, A. K. (2010). Length of stay for older adults residing in nursing homes at the end of life. *Journal of the American Geriatrics Society, 58*, 1701–1706. doi:10.1111/j.1532-5415.2010.03005.x.
30. Leitner, G., Felfernig, A., Fercher, A. J., & Hitz, M. (2014). Disseminating ambient assisted living in rural areas. *Sensors, Special Issue Ambient Assisted Living, 14*(8), 13496–13531.
31. Eurostat Yearbook. http://ec.europa.eu/eurostat/documents/3217494/5726181/KS-HA-10-001-15-EN.PDF/5499ee07-b61e-4615-9631-ed76e2a31f81?version=1.0.
32. Jonard, F., Lambotte, M., Ramos, F., Terres, J. M., & Bamps, C. (2009). *Delimitations of rural areas in Europe using criteria of population density, remoteness and land cover*. JRC Scientific and Technical Reports, European Commission, Joint Research Center, Institute for Environment and Sustainability (EUR, 23757).
33. Hirsch, T., Forlizzi, J., Hyder, E., Goetz, J., Kurtz, C., & Stroback, J. (2000). The ELDer project: Social, emotional, and environmental factors in the design of eldercare technologies. In *Proceedings on the 2000 Conference on Universal Usability* (pp. 72–79). New York: ACM.
34. Ahrens, M. (2009). Home fires involving cooking equipment. Quincy: National Fire Protection Association.
35. Nielsen, J. (1994). Heuristic evaluation. *Usability Inspection Methods, 17*(1), 25–62.
36. Leitner, G., Mitrea, O., & Fercher, A. J. (2013). Towards an acceptance model for AAL. In *Human factors in computing and informatics* (pp. 672–679). Berlin/Heidelberg: Springer.
37. Koskela, T., & Väänänen-Vainio-Mattila, K. (2004). Evolution towards smart home environments: Empirical evaluation of three user interfaces. *Personal and Ubiquitous Computing, 8*(3–4), 234–240.
38. Venkatesh, V., & Bala, H. (2008). Technology acceptance model 3 and a research agenda on interventions. *Decision Sciences, 39*(2), 273–315.
39. Beyer, H., & Holtzblatt, K. (1999). Contextual design. *Interactions, 6*(1), 32–42.
40. Scott, J. (2000). *Social network analysis: A handbook* (2nd ed.). London: Sage.
41. Gaver, B., Dunne, T., & Pacenti, E. (1999). Design: Cultural probes. *Interactions, 6*(1), 21–29.
42. Hamill, L. (2006). Controlling smart devices in the home. *The Information Society, 22*(4), 241–249.
43. Weiser, M. (1991). The computer for the 21st century. *Scientific American, 265*(3), 94–104.
44. Dourish, P. (2004). *Where the action is: The foundations of embodied interaction*. Cambridge: MIT.

Chapter 8
The WISE Future of Home Technology

This book started with the more-than-two-thousand year old ideas of Aristotle, describing the benefits of tools that could act on their own. In the following centuries many other essays can be found where this idea is repeated. Even in poetry, Goethe confronts his sorcerer's apprentice with such self-acting tools in the form of ghosts, however with the result that control over them is lost. It is not in our wishful thinking that tools act this way. The desirable alternative would be Mark Weiser's [1] technologies that interweave into our lives in such a way that using them would be: "*as refreshing as a walk in the woods*". It was illustrated throughout this book that today's technology has, fortunately, more or less overcome the level of the uncontrollable ghosts, but is, generally, still far from the status of interweaving itself into the environment. There are a few exceptions, such as the digital pen and paper combination that I mentioned in Chap. 7. It is one of the technologies that, in my opinion, point in the right direction. It shows how technology should be designed to enhance our lives without completely turning it upside down. Unfortunately, this is currently not the case with other technologies that can be assumed to have a higher relevance in our future, such as smart home technologies. The walk in the woods example from Weiser illustrates how an ecosystem should work and how interaction should take place. Everybody who has ever enjoyed such a walk would agree that the woods are full of information, and that they offer some means of interaction addressing all of our senses. Although the civilized human has unlearned several skills, most of us are able to enjoy the experience without becoming so distracted by the variety of stimuli that we are in danger of falling over a rock. The actions of the human are supported by diverse forms of feedback from the environment. For example, feedback that has been deliberately put in place by other humans: Consider feedback such as signposts or fences showing the correct direction and to preventing a walker from entering dangerous areas. But also more subtle information, such as trails that have obviously already been used by others, where the signs of their passage serve as signifiers to help us avoid unexpected

© Springer International Publishing Switzerland 2015
G. Leitner, *The Future Home is Wise, Not Smart*, Computer Supported
Cooperative Work, DOI 10.1007/978-3-319-23093-1_8

problems [2]. The characteristics of the woods, the possibility to peripherally experience the situation while also being able to focus on important tasks in parallel can be considered as a form of flow experience [3].

How is a situation different, when current technology is involved? It is not necessary to do intensive research to come across examples where technology failed to support a flow-like experience such as the nature experience emphasized above. Frequent reports can be found in the media about incidents caused by inappropriate technology, such as GPS devices misleading drivers. In contrast to the nature example, here the optimal combination of action and reaction between humans and the environment has obviously not been appropriately applied in technology. Mechanisms of peripheral attention, for example, as emphasized in Chap. 2, do not seem to be considered in the design of those devices. In contrast to the example of the middle hand bone that has evolved in about one million years evolution did not have enough time to adapt in a similar way to computerized technologies. In his book [4] showed, that multitasking and other parallelization of attentional processes does not seem to be possible for humans. When we fully concentrate on the information a GPS device is giving us, we do not have enough free resources to appropriately concentrate on other matters. The disruptiveness of technology is observable in people's use of smart phones [5]. It is difficult to estimate and understand what impact this form of technology may have in the future. All the same, [6] has provided a video which offers an outlook on a development which, in my opinion, is not desirable. Based on these examples, the worst case scenarios of home technologies in the future are anything but desirable. It seems to me that they make it clear that situated research with a focus on the non-technical aspects of smart home interaction has to be intensified.

Examples from other domains have been used because, as has been emphasized throughout this book, integrated and full-fledged smart homes do not yet have a high dissemination, and it is difficult to estimate how this will develop in the future. What is quite clear, in my opinion, is that the percentage of buildings in the functional building sector equipped with smart technology will increase, and the same is also true in those segments of the residential building sector where the buildings are established, managed and maintained by communities or cooperatives. In private and individual buildings, it is my opinion that the situation will probably be different. The decisions of private home-owners will depend on the costs and benefits related to the technologies, the channels where the devices are available, and the subjective estimation of whether or not they would be able to apply such technology (e.g. according to the dimensions of the TAM model [7]).

An indispensable prerequisite to prevent problems will be that there is some kind of standardization on the technical level, as has come to be the case with, for example, light bulbs which can be purchased anywhere and fitted with a high probability of success. Other similar developments, such as Plug&Play in the computer appliances sector, could also enhance consumer trust that components are at least physically compatible to their environment. These developments took a reasonable amount of time in other domains, but today devices meeting these standards can be trusted to install and configure themselves with a high probability. Similar developments would be prerequisite for an appropriate smart home technology of the future. As [8] pointed out, the role of system integrators will gain importance because, despite the benefits of handing over the responsibility for certain tasks to the end users, there would still be a need for qualified personnel to physically install the devices (e.g. because of security reasons). Our experiences in the projects described in this book is that, because of missing binding standards, following all of the trends in the market is as difficult for craftsmen as it is for end users. In the Casa Vecchia project described in Chap. 7, the majority of craftsmen we asked even advised end consumers against the adoption of smart technology because of the unstable situation regarding standards, and the resultant compatibility problems. For this reason, we can see that the craftsmen are another group involved in the situation that would benefit from a change towards a higher compatibility. Missing interoperability and compatibility are only two aspects contributing to a fear that the basic technology is not controllable. It seems that, as it was the case with the Japanese knotweed in gardening, that people are afraid that they would be in the mercy of technology and no more able to get rid of it. A major requirement for future technology is therefore to provide better means of control for the end user. This is supported by the idea of [9] who estimate that the era of *easy to develop* or *easy to program* technology, providing appropriate means to laypersons to enable them to adjust or create basic settings and to develop their own programs. Moreover, users also should be able to control their systems on their own and for their own purposes. They should be able to monitor their own privacy and security, and to control data transfer.

In times when we are frequently informed about who has access to all our data, how much information and data is transferred outside our homes, and how many devices such as smart TVs are spying on us, it is time to take back the control of the devices in our home. The following example illustrates the relevance of that idea. Around two years ago I was confronted by an issue that taught me just what kind of things could happen. It started with the problem that I had not been able to record a movie that was being broadcast by from the national public television station. The recording started, but was immediately interrupted without any message telling me what went wrong. I attributed the problem to technical issues, of the sort that this book is full of, and, with which all of us have become familiar since the introduction of the VCR. Who of us has ever been able to manage a recording which started and ended correctly, where no part of the program was missing and no additional contents such as advertisements were on the cassette? I have a good friend working with the broadcast station and he has another friend who is a technician with the company and therefore an expert in technical issues. As I am living in Carinthia and the both of them are in Vienna we do not see each other very often. But once we had the opportunity to go out together and, during the informal conversation, I asked the technician if he had any idea what the problem with my attempted recording might have been. What he told me both surprised and concerned me. I had not been able to record the program because the broadcast station sent a disruption signal to prevent it! It seems that I, as the consumer, do not have the right to record certain movies because of copyright issues. In addition to the fact that the broadcaster had the means to access and control my equipment, I had never been informed about these possibilities, or about the apparent fact that there are some rights problems with my intention to record a movie. Given the technical possibilities, it seems ridiculous when it happens that digital contents cannot be played on a certain device. Error messages such as *"This content is not available in your country"*, or *"This format is not supported by your device, driver is missing, wrong resolution, etc."* are not understandable. These are obviously not things that are restricted by technical limitations, but by product and service policies. It is not surprising in this regard that there were strong oppositions, specifically of organizations representing consumers, against the roll-out plans for smart meters in the European union. The resistance was not directed against measurement and data transfer in general, but against the intended standard procedure to automatically transfer all data to the energy provider, without giving the consumer the opportunity to observe and control the data leaving their household.

Automated functions similar to those we are used to with self-installing TVs or automatically-updating drivers on our computers, could help to ease the situation a lot. The WISE difference is that home-owners and dwellers are enabled to have the superiority of their own data and of their own equipment, and can control them with appropriate interfaces. It is natural that we do not hand over the responsibility of physical security of our homes to others. By the same principle, the average end consumer should also be enabled to take over responsibility for their virtual security.

That even complex tasks are reasonable even for average consumers is demonstrated on one exemplary work which was carried out in the context of the WISE home by [10], who developed a smart home configurator tool (Fig. 8.1). The tool enables lay persons to sketch a floorplan of their own living environment and position devices and pieces of furniture present in the home. In the back-end the components required to make the sketched home smart are calculated and shown to the user in the form of a parts list. The concept is based on the Drag&Drop prototype presented in Chap. 7.

The initial step which could enable end consumers to configure their homes could also enable them to control their homes in a better way. The Drag&Drop concept on which [10]s prototype is based is also the basic concept of the scenario programming example [11] presented in Chap. 7. In this regard I would not fully agree to the statements of [12] regarding the wish to be a system administrator in the home. They were emphasizing that the willingness to take over the responsibility and the efforts of administering and maintaining a smart home is low. But this is only one perspective, based on the entirely valid concerns about the basic technology and how the procedures are done today. But this situation may change. I have shed a spotlight on some of the developments in technology in the home over the last decades and I have also touched on video processing. In the past it has been quite cumbersome to record video, edit it and distribute it in a reasonable quality. Today, with smart phones, this is no longer a problem. Within a few seconds videos are recorded and shared world-wide, all without a problem. And people are interested in and willing to use these features because they feel that they are able to do the task and that these features enrich their lives in some way. If there were appropriate technologies

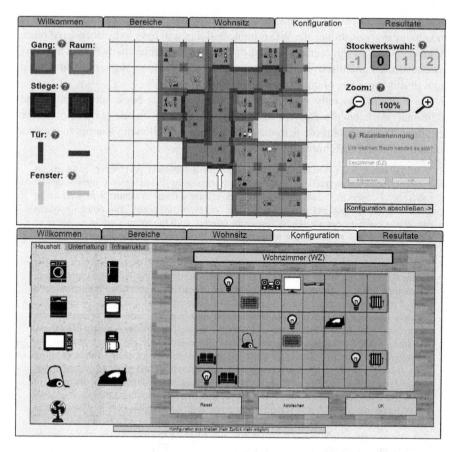

Fig. 8.1 WISE home configurator [10] – the prototype enables users to configure their own smart home system on the basis of a floor plan that can be established with Drag&Drop. Devices present in the home can be placed in the floor plan, and a recommender/configurator system in the backend calculates the components (actuators/sensors) that are needed to make the home smart in the first step, and WISE with the appropriate superstructure

in a home things may also change and not develop as currently anticipated. Many examples throughout history showed that these changes are possible. To mention only two, in 1927, Harry Warner of Warner Brothers Studios asked who would want to hear actors talk. In 1943, Thomas Watson from IBM estimated that there would only ever be a world market for five computers. Given the importance of the home in our lives and the time [13] that we spend there, we would all probably be more than happy to invest some effort into the goal of leading a good life......if the technology to do so were appropriate.

The examples presented in Chap. 7 show that the WISE concept is flexible and open enough to support further activities in this direction. However, it is not a finished concept, but one that continues to evolve. The things that were illustrated throughout the book can be considered as exploratory drilling for a big deposit of knowledge that constitutes the WISE home and that will have to be uncovered piece by piece. Some of the corner stones are already observable, many others have yet to be identified and discovered by appropriate research. One of the most important areas in this regard is, of course, wisdom.

The concept has only been touched throughout this book superficially, and additional work on the concept and its relevance will be the subject of future activities. The basis of those activities builds from the following attempt to create a definition of the WISE home.

A WISE home is an environment constituting of a technical part which is based on different technologies such as conventional technologies (white goods, brown goods) and general connecting technologies (network infrastructures, computers) as well as on specific smart components that serve a broad variety of purposes. The other important part of the environment are the humans who interact with the technology in a variety of ways. Those forms of interaction are categorized across two principle dimensions, called explicit interaction and implicit interaction. The former is characterized by the provision of appropriate, multi-modal and adaptive interfaces which enable users to interact with the technical part of the WISE home according to their needs and preferences in a voluntary and explicit form. In is important that this form of interaction is prioritized over the second form of interaction, implicit interaction. By implicit interaction we mean that a human does not have to interact with a physical device or an interface. The technical system accepts interaction in the form of behaviours and derives information and functionality from them. The basis for these features are ambient intelligence technologies, which: can analyze behaviour, can identify routines or patterns, and can derive automated functions from them. Information about basic processes, derived assumptions and proposed functionality is conveyed to the humans with appropriate interfaces, for example with dialogues or alternative interface design concepts such as informative art. With these basic components and concepts the WISE home system has the possibility to support people with different needs, user preferences, and requirements. The system is adaptive on different levels. It is also able to cope with changes in hardware without having to exchange the whole system. It also is able to deal with changes to the social aspects (e.g. family constellation, changes related to age, etc.) and their consequences.

As an example, in the living environment of a young couple, a WISE home system would support comfort aspects – enabling the most flexible control of devices, from smart phones or tablets, for example. In a family constellation, where children are present, the system changes to the requirement of a larger number of users, anticipates or reacts to potential conflicts, covers security issues (in terms of childrens physical safety with dangerous devices, as well as their mental or emotional safety in terms of potentially dangerous content and functions (Internet, Television)). In order to deal with higher energy consumption, the system automatically observes energy usage behaviour, informs the inhabitants, and provides the possibility to intervene. When people are older, or when they have to deal with changes in health, the WISE home supports their needs, enhances the security functions, and is able to integrate friends or relatives living outside in order to be able to provide remote support.

As the variety is big, I want to give an example of what I would understand by a really WISE home. As mentioned several times throughout this book, the home is a sensible ecosystem and people do not want to be disturbed in their goal to lead a good life. An example for a feature that I frequently wish for is related to the currently distributed devices and services in a household and the digital contents that are available. When I am writing (such as is the case right now) this is typically done in front of a computer, at the moment in the office at the university, but also possible in my home office or one some other desk in my house. When I have finished a part or the whole document it is saved, for example as a PDF. After writing, many review cycles are necessary. Reviewing can be done visually, either on the computer or on a printout. I consider myself an *acoustic* person and, in some cases, I enjoy listening to documents instead of reading them. I can manage this with more or less any document with the help of text-to-speech software programs. But there are several drawbacks with the current situation that could be resolved with a really WISE technology in the home, combining implicit and explicit interaction and multi-modality. Currently, I have to think myself that I have to transcode the .pdf file to an .mp3 file and to store it on a device or a cloud storage that the content is accessible from elsewhere to be able to listen to it. A WISE home could probably extract automated patterns from my behaviour and enhance my experience a lot.

Sometimes it is the case that I go to bed after writing with the plan to do reviewing there. When my wife is awake it is no problem to take the e-book reader and read the document recently written (with additional lights or without) after having accessed it in the cloud. When my wife has already fallen asleep the manipulation of the e-book reader would wake her up. The most unobtrusive way of *reading* a document would be to *listen* to it. On the technical level, this would not be a problem, if I had not forgotten to manually transcode the file into .mp3. However, the handling of the streaming client is based on visual and tactile interaction. I have to search the menu hierarchy to select the file on the cloud storage, and this would wake up my wife. Currently all the preparation would have to be done beforehand.

A really WISE solution would be if the system (where all of my devices are integrated) recognizes a typical pattern, or is able to react spontaneously to commands given in a different modality. This could be done on the basis of components that are already available in a conventional home, for example motion sensors. The preferred variant would be the following. When I go to bed and I were to recognize that my wife is asleep, I would not switch on the lights. I would put on the headset and, in my softest voice, would whisper "*recent*". As has been shown in the work with [14] it would be quite easy for a real smart home system to respond by following all of the required steps. The system is aware that I am not using a visual device. With the command "*recent*" it would scan my recent activities (similar to functions offered in diverse software programs, but across different devices) and find the recently-saved document on my office computer. Recognizing that the document is in PDF and that I would not be able to view it in the current context the system would automatically transcode it to an audio file and play it to me – all without disturbing anyone else. If I would like to change the file, I could interact with the motion sensor, since there are already some of them installed in the home as a part of the alarm system. I should be able to use it to navigate through my files. What I want to point out with this example is that some of current technical possibilities would already be sufficient so support needs. In many cases it would only be necessary to take better consideration of requirements. But these can only be observed in situated research. A major criticism that could be made of my work and also of this book is that the things that I describe are mainly addressed from a subjective viewpoint. I want to answer this with the words of [15]. He points out that in research there is typically a tendency towards quantitative data, quantification, replication – while subjective aspects are often seen as irrelevant. The question is, what if the subjective is the more important one? Then the approach focused on quantifiable parameters would fail. In my opinion, this is one of the reasons that smart home technology is still trending behind the expected curve. Other forms of research are required, which have long traditions in philosophy, as can been seen in the phenomenology, in sociology, and which experience a revival in HCI with *embodiement* [16–18]. Only research that also addresses the subjective – the situated perspective – can truly identify complex aspects of living such as *values*. The WISE approach aims to contribute to the idea that technology better fits into life, or – with the words of Weiser – is enabled to *interweave* with it. According to [19] is wisdom a *rather optional* stage of development, speaking of humans. But although wisdom in the home is also optional, it is still worth it to follow the idea.

References

1. Weiser, M. (1991). The computer for the 21st century. *Scientific American, 265*(3), 94–104.
2. Norman, D. A. (2010). *Living with complexity.* Cambridge: MIT.
3. Nakamura, J., & Csikszentmihalyi, M. (2002). The concept of flow. In *Handbook of positive psychology* (pp. 89–105). Oxford/New York: Oxford University Press.
4. Medina, J. (2008). *Brain rules: 12 principles for surviving and thriving at work, home, and school.* Seattle: Pear Press.
5. Ling, R. (2004). *The mobile connection: The cell phone's impact on society.* Burlington: Morgan Kaufmann.
6. de Guzman, C. (2013). I forgot my phone. https://www.youtube.com/watch?v=OINa46HeWg8.
7. Venkatesh, V., & Bala, H. (2008). Technology acceptance model 3 and a research agenda on interventions. *Decision Sciences, 39*(2), 273–315.
8. Barlow, J., & Gann, D. (1998) A changing sense of place: Are integrated IT systems reshaping the home? http://139.184.32.141/Units/spru/publications/imprint/sewps/sewp18/sewp18.pdf.
9. Lieberman, H., Paternó, F., Klann, M., & Wulf, V. (2006). *End-user development: An emerging paradigm* (pp. 1–8). Amsterdam: Springer.
10. Pum, M. *Configurator-Umgebung für die Unterstützung der Erstellung individualisierter Smarthome Systeme.* Diploma Thesis, Alpen-Adria Universität Klagenfurt. Work in Progress.
11. Leitner, G., Fercher, A. J., & Lassen, C. (2013). End users programming smart homes – A case study on scenario programming. In *Human-computer interaction and knowledge discovery in complex, unstructured, big data* (pp. 217–236). Berlin/Heidelberg: Springer.
12. Edwards, W. K., & Grinter, R. E. (2001). At home with ubiquitous computing: Seven challenges. In *Ubicomp: Ubiquitous computing* (pp. 256–272). Berlin/Heidelberg: Springer.
13. Hamill, L. (2006). Controlling smart devices in the home. *The Information Society, 22*(4), 241–249.

14. Brown, J. N. A. (2014). *Unifying interaction across distributed controls in a smart environment using anthropology-based computing to make human-computer interaction "Calm".* Ph.D. Thesis, Erasmus Mundus Doctorate Program in Interactive and Cognitive Environments (ICE), Alpen Adria Universität Klagenfurt, Austria.
15. King, P. (2004). Private dwelling: Contemplating the use of housing. London/New York: Psychology Press.
16. Heidegger, M. (1952). Bauen Wohnen Denken. Vorträge und Aufsätze (p. 151).
17. Jahoda, M., Lazarsfeld, P. F., & Zeisel, H. (1960). *Die Arbeitslosen von Marienthal: ein soziographischer Versuch über die Wirkungen langandauernder Arbeitslosigkeit, mit einem Anhang zur Geschichte der Soziographie* (Vol. 2). Allensbach: Verlag für Demoskopie.
18. Dourish, P. (2004). *Where the action is: The foundations of embodied interaction.* Cambridge: MIT.
19. Staudinger, U. M., & Glück, J. (2011). Psychological wisdom research: Commonalities and differences in a growing field. *Annual Review of Psychology, 62,* 215–241.

Epilogue

A "WISE" birthday speculation.

Some years from now I will participate in an event where an extended family meets to celebrate a 50th birthday. Technology will play an important role in the celebration, however, it will do so in a manner nobody can anticipate today. The following example illustrates the possibilities of the technology that will be present in an future home, and what might make it really smart, or even WISE. *In the late afternoon, all of the family members (17 adults, because the children of the first story have long since grown up, and two children) meet in the living room. Because of the special event, additional devices are present, enhancing the technical equipment that is typically available. In summary, there are several digital cameras, a video camcorder, a dozen smart phones, a musical keyboard, a tablet, a TV, a blue-ray player present in the room. After the meal the guests will start chatting about this and that and the discussion will come around a holiday trip that one couple will have taken a few weeks earlier. Of course the couple is prepared to show pictures. As usual in the future, the pictures will not be available as a physical photo album, but on the storage card in one of the digital cameras or already in a cloud storage. One half of the couple simply puts the camera on top of the TV set, and the TV automatically starts a slide show mode which can be easily configured with any remote control that is available in the house, because they are all based on a similar and intuitive interaction concept. The home system recognizes that the lighting conditions to view pictures are not optimal and adjusts the blinds automatically. For those who are interested, and who have standard equipment at home, a selection of photos is burned onto a blue ray and given to them. For the others, a selection of photos is loaded on their own cloud storage where they can be viewed from their preferred location and device. As a grandmother is short sighted, she would want to view the photos in another way. The photos are transferred by a gesture to her tablet, and grandmother can flip through them on the ancient photo album app installed there just for her. To shorten the story, the whole audience can see the*

© Springer International Publishing Switzerland 2015

G. Leitner, *The Future Home is Wise, Not Smart*, Computer Supported Cooperative Work, DOI 10.1007/978-3-319-23093-1 *photos simultaneously and, if wanted, the TV provides additional information on the location where the journey took place on the basis of mining the conversation of the present people for keywords. The technology present will integrate itself in the scene in such an unintrusive way that the experience will be so immersive and smart that it will seem as though the whole family had been on holiday themselves.*

Printed in the United States
By Bookmasters